The Ghosts of
Thua Thien

The Ghosts of Thua Thien

An American Soldier's Memoir of Vietnam

JOHN A. NESSER

McFarland & Company, Inc., Publishers

Jefferson, North Carolina, and London

LIBRARY OF CONGRESS CATALOGUING-IN-PUBLICATION DATA

Nesser, John A, 1946–
    The ghosts of Thua Thien : an American soldier's
memoir of Vietnam / John A. Nesser.
        p.   cm.
    Includes index.

    ISBN 978-0-7864-3324-7
    softcover : 50# alkaline paper ∞

    1. Vietnam War, 1961–1975 — Personal narratives, American.
2. Vietnam War, 1961–1975 — Psychological aspects.   3. Nesser,
John A., 1946–   I. Title.
DS559.5.N47   2008
959.704'3092 — dc22   2007052123

British Library cataloguing data are available

Cover photograph: Combat Assault near the DMZ

Manufactured in the United States of America

*McFarland & Company, Inc., Publishers
    Box 611, Jefferson, North Carolina 28640
    www.mcfarlandpub.com*

For Linda
My transition from war to family life would not have
been possible without your love, patience and understanding.

Acknowledgments

I want to thank Henry Shovic, Ph.D., for his review of this book. His insights and suggestions were vital in helping me to clearly express my thoughts about Vietnam.

My longtime friend, Michael Dumas, also asked helpful questions and offered valuable suggestions. I thank him as well.

Finally, I would like to thank my wife, Linda, and my two sons, Tim and Joe. Their review provided me with personal insights and helped me to remember details that I had forgotten.

Contents

Contents

Introduction

I spent my entire Vietnam tour of duty in Thua Thien Province except for a memorable combat assault near the DMZ (demilitarized zone). The Thua Thien area of operations was the scene of some of the heaviest fighting in the war, and more men became casualties there than anywhere else in Vietnam. The enemy soldiers we were fighting often seemed like ghosts in the thick jungle, and those ghosts still haunt me many years later — hence the title of this book. This is a personal narrative recounting my tour of duty with the 101st Airborne Division as both an infantry rifleman and Chinook helicopter door gunner in and above the mountainous jungles in northern South Vietnam. Though my experience may have been typical of many young men who were drafted and served their country, it is also very personal. Like every soldier, I saw and experienced the events of war through my own eyes, drew my own conclusions, and live with the memories.

The Vietnam War produced its share of extraordinary men, men who were involved in major battles and saw some of the worst fighting imaginable. The 1st Air Cavalry Division's famous fight in the Ia Drang Valley, the Marines' siege at Khe San, and the 101st Airborne Division's battle for Hamburger Hill in the Ashau Valley all come to my mind. That same war was also responsible for self-proclaimed heroes, members of fictitious military units begging on street corners and a multitude of myths and urban legends that are still believed and accepted by many people. This book is not about heroes or famous battles, and it is not a political statement on the war — with the exception of a few personal thoughts. It is not a work of fiction or a description of myths. I was in Vietnam from May 1969, to July 1970. I lived there every day. This is my story, the story of an unforgettable year in my life.

While I was in Vietnam I wrote to my wife nearly every day, at least when I had the opportunity. She saved every letter that I wrote, and when I returned home in July 1970, she showed me the box containing all the letters. Shortly thereafter, whether in a fit of anger or as a gesture that in my mind freed me from what I had just experienced, I burned every letter, one by one, in the kitchen sink. As I write this book, I now wish that I had those letters. They represented actual, almost day-by-day accounts of everything that I experienced or thought about in Vietnam. Instead, I have been forced to rely on my somewhat aging memory to recall events and thoughts that occurred over 35 years ago, many of which I suppressed for many years after I returned from Vietnam. Some of those events are indelibly etched into my memory, while my recollection of other happenings is more vague and elusive. I have attempted to portray the accounts in this book as accurately as I remember them, but the chronological order may not always be precise. I should also point out that this book describes some of the more memorable incidents that took place during my tour of duty. I have mostly forgotten the lonely, endless days, the drudgery, misery, and boredom. They are distant memories now. Someone once said that war is mostly endless boredom punctuated by moments of absolute terror. I remember the terror.

Any errors in describing places or events are unintentional and are entirely mine. I have chosen to use fictitious names and not to identify the brave young men I served with in order to protect their privacy. Unfortunately, I cannot even recall all of their names. I have chosen to include the term "gooks" in this book only for historical accuracy and authenticity. It was a commonly used term for the enemy during the Vietnam War. I do not intend to demean the Vietnamese or any Asian people in any way, and I apologize to anyone who is offended.

Prologue

My conservative, middle-class Catholic upbringing in the small, central Wisconsin town of Marshfield during the late 1950s and early 1960s was typical midwest Americana. In grade school our teachers talked about the evils of Communism, and we were instructed to hide under our desks in case of a nuclear attack. I knew almost nothing about Vietnam and could not have found it on a map. Our geography text described it as French Indochina but said little else. My high school history teacher talked about Dr. Tom Dooley's book, *Deliver Us From Evil,* and played a tape of one of his speeches for us. She read passages from his book that described the atrocities that were being committed by the Vietnamese Communists. I learned later that Dooley often sensationalized his accounts to further United States political aims in Southeast Asia. The United States' involvement in Vietnam was just starting then, but my friends and I were far too busy playing football and chasing girls to worry about it or even pay attention to the news. Besides, we thought that we were all going to college, so the prospect of getting drafted just did not mean anything.

The early 1960s were magical years for me, and I thought I had the world by the tail. I was emerging from adolescence into adulthood, and the music, counterculture movement, and my plans for college all coalesced to give me a feeling of freedom and invincibility. Little did I realize then that events in a small country in Southeast Asia would soon destroy my youth and change my life forever.

My dad was the local newspaper editor, and I shared a very close

3

relationship with him. He was a handsome man with dark hair whom his friends had nicknamed "Blackie" even though his real name was Larry. A graduate of Marquette University in Milwaukee, he had degrees in both journalism and philosophy and could always be counted on to expound on politics and life in general. We spent long hours discussing the Vietnam War, though we did not always come to the same conclusions. Dad was supportive of the Vietnam War mostly because he liked President Johnson and hated the idea of Communism. I was not sure that our involvement in the war was the right course of action, but at the same time, I had no respect for the anti-war movement. Dad shared his philosophy and wisdom with me and became the most influential man in my life; I loved him and respected him deeply. He was a patriotic man with courage and tenacity. During World War II he attempted to enlist in the Marine Corps and almost succeeded in taking the oath before a doctor discovered that he was totally deaf in one ear. That disqualified him from serving in the military. Since he could not enlist in the Marine Corps, he went to work in a defense plant in Milwaukee, and during that time he met and married my mother.

My mom was a diminutive woman, a very devout Catholic who taught all of us our lessons in faith from the time we began to walk. I recall going to Sunday mass with her and Dad every week, and she would often take me to Tuesday services as well. She made sure we all did well in school and provided us with a moral foundation. She was not a student of world affairs, however, so she said very little about Vietnam to me. Mom was a somewhat naive person, a gentle soul whom I loved deeply.

I acquired my dad's love for the outdoors, which led me to pursue the study of natural resources in college. During my first three years at the University of Wisconsin in Stevens Point, I stayed with my aunt Georgia, who also shared many interests with me, including hikes in the woods and wildlife observation. She was a jolly, rotund lady who was always playing practical jokes, and she seemed almost like a second mother to me. I remember watching the Vietnam War news on television every night during supper and wondering if it would be over before I graduated and my college draft deferment terminated. Aunt

Georgia and I did not discuss the war very often, and I didn't have strong feelings against the war. I often wondered, however, if the United States had made a major foreign policy blunder by getting involved. A small group of anti-war protesters gathered every Saturday morning in front of the Post Office with their peace signs and their leader, an English professor. Even though I sympathized with them on an intellectual level, my patriotic feelings caused me to consider them to be either misguided, misinformed, or Communist sympathizers. Like many young men during that era, I had deep internal conflicts about the war. During that time, just before the draft lottery began, men were deferred from the draft while they were in college. As graduation approached I became more and more uneasy about getting drafted, but I did not come up with any clear solutions to that dilemma. There did not seem to be any end in sight to the rapidly escalating war in Vietnam, and the casualty list was growing every week. After reading several books on the history of Vietnam, I became even more convinced that the United States had made a mistake by entering the war.

In the summer between my junior and senior years in college I married my sweetheart, Linda, and we began to make plans for our future. During my senior year, I considered applying to either the Air Force or Naval Officer Candidate School (OCS). Either branch of the service was highly preferable to being drafted into the Army as far as I could tell, and I went to Milwaukee to take a physical and talk to the recruiters. The Air Force OCS seemed particularly interesting because they had a career field that fit nicely into my college specialization in geography and mapping. That career field was filled up, however, and the Air Force was only recruiting pilots. Unfortunately, I did not qualify for flight training because my eyesight was less than perfect. The Naval OCS also seemed interesting, but I missed the qualification test by a few points the first time I took it. Very foolishly, I never bothered to try again and retake the test. I guess I was not anxious to begin our marriage with a four-year stint in the military, so the idea of enlisting eventually got dropped. Besides, we had a baby on the way, and I had received a job offer to work as a geographer with the Army Map Service in Washington, D.C., after I graduated in June 1968. When I graduated I also lost my student deferment, but I thought that somehow I

5

would not be drafted because I was working for the Department of the Army, though as a civilian. Many young men in college talked about going to Canada or otherwise dodging the draft, but I never really considered that option. My conservative upbringing had instilled in me a strong sense of duty to my country, and I would never have risked the disapproval of my family, especially my dad, who was my model and hero.

Our son, Tim, was born on July 15, 1968, and in early August I packed up our 1963 Chevrolet Impala and headed for Rockville, Maryland. I planned to stay with my uncle Clyde until I found an apartment and Linda and Tim could join me. I embraced my new job and enjoyed working on classified maps of various foreign countries. Uncle Clyde advised me to change my draft board registration from Wisconsin to the board in Washington, D.C., since it had a much larger pool of potential draftees. In theory, that would have decreased the odds of being drafted, but I neglected to make the change. Instead, I left my fate up to the local draft board in Wood County, Wisconsin, not realizing that my days as a civilian were numbered.

Early in September, I picked Linda and Tim up at Washington National Airport, and we began our life as a family. We enjoyed the history and the national monuments in Washington, D.C., and spent nearly every weekend visiting historical sites. My uncle lived close to us and offered support as we settled into a comfortable lifestyle. I began to enjoy my work, and we started to make friends with other young families that we met through my work connections. The Vietnam War seemed very far away, and we gave it very little thought.

"Above all, Vietnam was a war that asked everything
of a few and nothing of most in America."
— Myra MacPherson, 1984

And the end of the fight
Is tombstone white
With the name of the late deceased,
And the epitaph drear,
"A fool lies here
Who tried to hustle the East."
— Rudyard Kipling

1

Drafted

It was a chilly day in late October, 1968. I had just received my draft notice in the mail and had been ordered to report to the military induction center in Milwaukee, Wisconsin, on December 5. I stood looking out of the window and watched the rain trickle down the windowpane as I contemplated my future. Linda was crying and I was in shock as I stared again at the draft notice as if it might all be a dream. I should have seen it coming but just did not want to believe that I would be among those who would be selected to serve. My mind began to wander as the prospect of being in the army and going to war hit me square in the face. I would soon become part of a brotherhood of warriors that dated back to the armies of Alexander the Great, Genghis Khan, and many others throughout history. The life that Linda and I had just begun was turned upside down in a few short moments that day.

There were plenty of things to do before we were ready to return to Wisconsin. I had paperwork to complete at work before I was ready to check out and hand in my security badge. I felt really sad at having to leave my new job so soon and all the friends we had made in the short time we resided in the Washington, D.C., area. Luckily we had not signed a lease and leaving our apartment was not a problem. Within a week we packed our clothes and other belongings into the Chevy and said hasty goodbyes to my uncle and the friends we had made during our brief stay in suburban Maryland. Our hearts were about as heavy as the loaded-down car when we began our journey back to Wisconsin. Our plans were to have Linda and Tim stay with her family after I reported to the induction center in Milwaukee to be inducted into the army. The trip to Wisconsin was about as gloomy as the early November weather, and our mood was not upbeat. I was very nervous about the unknown scenario that was playing out before our eyes and I withdrew into my inner thoughts. Linda cried a lot, and I kept thinking about everything I should have done but did not. It was too late to do anything now because the machinery that would drive my fate had been set in motion and I could not change or stop it.

November seemed to go by quickly and I worked to get Linda and Tim settled. I wanted to get everything in order so they did not have to worry while I was gone. We made several trips from Marshfield to Neillsville where Linda's folks lived. She and Tim would be staying with them while I was gone and we moved most of our belongings to their house. I went deer hunting with my dad in northern Wisconsin late in November. I had gone deer hunting with my dad since I was 16 and it had become an anticipated annual event for both of us. It was different this time and my heart was not in it. Carrying my rifle only served to further remind me of what lay ahead of me. My dad and I did a lot of talking, which helped both of us sort things out. Though he didn't say it, I could tell that he was worried about me and he kept telling me to be aware of my surroundings and watch my back. I assured him that I would be extra cautious though we both knew that complete control over one's fate is not possible. When I returned from the hunting trip, I drew up a will just in case I did not make it home. Even though I had not been assigned anywhere yet, I knew in my heart that I was going to Vietnam.

On December 4, 1968, I boarded a Greyhound bus in front of the Hotel Charles in Marshfield and watched Linda and my parents wave goodbye as the bus pulled away. The snowy, overcast day only added to the gloomy feeling I had as we headed for Milwaukee. The five-hour ride seemed to last forever as I mulled over the events that had preceded my current predicament. Again, I thought of all the things I should have done. If I had gone into teaching or engineering in college, I might have escaped induction because those fields were pretty much exempt from the draft, or at least it appeared that way. It was now far too late to change anything. I was going to be in the army, and even though I would not let myself admit it, I knew where I was going. When I got to Milwaukee, I was assigned to a room in a run-down hotel near the induction center along with about 20 or 30 other men. We were told to report to the center at 0700 hours the next morning. December 5 turned out to be a very long and stressful day. After running a gauntlet of protesters who were handing out literature just outside the induction center, we began our processing. As we entered the building, several men in uniform promptly confiscated the literature we were given by the protesters. They tossed it into a large trash container and began barking orders. Everyone seemed to be confused. I endured a battery of physical exams as well as an army aptitude test. Most of us realized that we were headed for Vietnam as infantry riflemen and we viewed the aptitude test as a sham. The processing went on for most of the day, and after completing the aptitude and other tests and passing all of the physical examinations, a group of us were led into a small room. There, we raised our right hands, took an oath, and were inducted into the U.S. Army. Next, we were bused to Billy Mitchell Field and put aboard an airplane that would transport us to Fort Campbell in Kentucky for basic training. I could hardly believe that I was actually headed for basic training in the army as I stared out into the night sky and watched the city lights fade as we left Milwaukee. The flight to Fort Campbell was fairly short, and I soon saw a snowy landscape below as we approached the airfield and circled to land. The snow surprised me because I had always thought of Kentucky as a warm southern state.

After we landed a bus took us to the reception center and our life in the army began in earnest. About an hour later a clerk assigned to training platoons, and DIs (drill instructors) wearing flat-brimmed hats marched us to our barracks. They yelled at us constantly and did their best to intimidate us, deliberately creating a sense of chaos. The senior DI was a large black man with a fierce look in his eyes. He set the tone for our training when he glared at one young man with long hair and yelled, "Son, you better give your soul to Jesus, because your ass is mine!"

The barracks were drafty old World War II–era white wooden

two-story buildings lined up in neat rows around a large snow-covered parade field. They seemed to sprawl forever and the stark monotony was depressing. Finally, after what seemed like hours, we picked up sheets and wool blankets from the supply shack near our barracks and every man was assigned to a bunk. I got an upper bunk, which was great because it was cold in the barracks and there was a draft near the floor. My lower bunkmate was a black trainee from Milwaukee, and we hit it off right away. He and I turned out to be close friends, though I never saw him again after basic training. Even though we were very tired, most of us did not sleep very well that first night, and quiet conversations continued at length until most of the men drifted off into an uneasy sleep.

Early the next day we began our processing into the army. At 0400 hours the DI woke everyone up by yelling and beating on a garbage can with a wooden stick. Several men did not hop out of bed right away, and they soon found themselves sprawled on the floor along with their mattresses and bedding. The scene was mass confusion as recruits fought to take care of bathroom chores and shave, then get dressed and stand in formation in front of the barracks. We stood shivering in the cold in our thin civilian clothes since we had not yet been issued our army fatigues and other clothing. The DI looked at one man who was not wearing a jacket and said, "Why are you shivering, Numb-nuts? Did you think you were coming to the sunny south?" After a brief inspection and harassment, we were marched to the chow hall, where we had pancakes and sausage for breakfast. After being hurried out of the chow hall, we were marched to the supply shack and were issued all of our fatigues and other gear. Since it was winter in Kentucky, the issue included a field jacket, a cap with ear flaps, gloves, and long underwear. One of the first things our DI did on our march from clothing supply to our barracks was to make us dump all of our new gear on the muddy parade field and march back and forth until it was ground into the mud. Then we all had to find our gear in the mud, retrieve it and march back to the barracks. After we dressed in our new fatigues, we spent about an hour doing physical training and running around the parade field in the snow. Later that morning we marched over to a barber shop not too far from our company area and were told that we could request any type of haircut we desired. Some of the less savvy recruits actually told the barbers how they'd like their hair cut. Of course, we all received the infamous "trainee traditional" haircut, which amounted to having our heads nearly shaved. The rest of the day was spent learning how to line up properly and how to march. After evening chow was finished, we spent most of the rest of the night cleaning our clothes in the sinks and showers in order to be ready for inspection the next morning.

The DIs spent most of the next few weeks teaching a bunch of civilians how to line up straight and march. We seemed to run constantly and do physical training at least two or three times a day. The army's objective was to get us in physical shape, develop our confidence, and divorce us from our civilian identities. The methods used were often severe. We got some sort of immunization every week: shots for typhoid, tetanus, yellow fever, cholera, plague, and other diseases I had never realized existed. The DIs called most of the trainees "numb-nuts" or some other derogatory name. Profanity was almost universal, and I learned phrases and curses that were new to me. Many recruits had to endure verbal assaults on their masculinity and were called faggots, fairies, queers, girls, and more colorful names. A recruit's intelligence was not immune from verbal attack either, and I quickly learned that the DIs had a very low regard for "college boys," whom they singled out as scapegoats for just about everything. Working long hours in the kitchen or mess hall and scrubbing out latrines was considered especially appropriate work for anyone who had attended college.

The training class was a mixture of high school kids who had enlisted and a number of draftees like myself, many of whom had attended or graduated from college. It seemed that about every third day all of the trainees who had graduated from college were marched over to a small white building and were lectured and strongly encouraged to sign up for OCS (Officer Candidate School). The usual pitch was that if we signed up, we would be getting out of basic training class, would have opportunities for great assignments, and would be treated like gentlemen rather than recruits. I considered signing up for OCS, but it would have required an extra year in the army. I heard through the rumor mill, like everyone else, that becoming a second lieutenant would mean an almost certain assignment to Vietnam as an infantry platoon leader. The rumor mill also had it that second lieutenants were usually killed within one month after going to Vietnam. That did not seem like a particularly great option to me at the time, so I said "no thanks." As I would find out later, the rumor mills were not very accurate and not signing up for OCS was a big mistake. Officers usually spent six months in the field, while the enlisted men were often in front-line units in the field for their entire one-year tour of duty.

Just before Christmas, basic training was shut down and everyone was issued a pass and sent home on a two-week leave. I boarded a bus and headed back to Marshfield, where I was greeted by Linda and Tim when the bus pulled up in front of Hotel Charles. I was really looking forward to spending Christmas with everyone and it was great to be home, even for two weeks. I tried not to think about Fort Campbell, but that was impossible. It was depressing to think about returning to Fort Campbell for more basic training, and those thoughts put a damper on my enthusiasm during the holidays. Linda and I made the best of it, and the break gave us a chance to relax and enjoy our families. Unfortunately, my two-week leave went by all too fast.

On January 2, 1969, I stood in front of Hotel Charles, smelling the diesel fumes from the idling Greyhound bus and saying goodbye to everyone again. This time, however, as I boarded the bus for the return trip to Fort Campbell, I had some company. A friend with whom I had attended high school had also been drafted, and by sheer luck we both ended up in the same basic training company. We had not been close friends in school, but Mike and I had bonded during the first two weeks of basic training and traveling back together made it a little easier for both of us. We spent most of the trip to Fort Campbell talking about training, discussing the DIs, and speculating as to whether or not ours would be the lucky graduating class that would be sent to Germany and not to Vietnam.

After our return to Fort Campbell, training resumed with a vengeance. The marching and physical training escalated, and it seemed that the DIs had gotten more brutal over the holidays. Their job, as they put it, was to take a bunch of civilians, misfits, and losers and mold them into a lean, mean fighting machine. They were good at what they did and army training, as far as it went, was very effective. It was based on endless repetition and physical threats. Not only were the DIs training us physically to be soldiers, they were messing with our minds. We were being indoctrinated with the idea that "killing is fun," "the spirit of the bayonet is to kill without mercy," and that "we wanted to go to Vietnam to kill gooks." I hated the vulgarity and silently protested by mouthing the words but not saying them out loud unless there was a DI within earshot. They had us believing that NVA (North Vietnamese Army) and VC (Viet Cong) soldiers were somehow superhuman and very evil. All Vietnamese people were referred to as "gooks," mostly out of ignorance, but there was also deliberate design to the racist terminology. Obviously, if you depersonalize and dehumanize an enemy soldier, it is much easier to kill him. The army did a marvelous job of indoctrinating the younger recruits, but many of the older men like me, especially draftees, were not as malleable and did not buy into all the gung-ho bullshit. That made no difference to the DIs and they never ceased the endless indoctrination.

The winter weather in Kentucky was cold and humid, making our training miserable and adding to both our physical and mental discomfort. It was cold in the barracks at night, and I usually slept in my long underwear and wore a stocking cap. We spent early mornings shivering in the chow line outside the mess hall waiting for breakfast. The food was tolerable, but before we could eat we had to low-crawl through the snow and ice for about 50 feet and then swing on parallel bars for another 30 feet in order to earn our way into the mess hall. The DIs screamed at us constantly and there was no such thing as an enjoyable meal. Our platoon DI who about 30 years old and not as loud or demeaning as most of the other DIs. I liked him because he treated us fairly and seemed to have some empathy for what we were experiencing. He seemed to like me and was one of a few DIs who treated me with some respect. He often gave me important advice and encouragement, which I appreciated.

Since the barracks were old and were considered to be firetraps, each man took his turn at fireguard duty for two hours during the night. Considering the number of men in each platoon, each man got his turn in the rotation about every third night. The man on duty patrolled the building, both inside and out, to check for potential hazards and to make sure that the building was secure. I did not mind fireguard duty at night because it gave me a lot of time to think about Linda and Tim and make plans for the future. Otherwise, basic training dragged on day after day.

I will always remember one humorous incident that occurred on a march back from training one rainy day. We had been wearing our ponchos, and shortly after the march began it quit raining. We were given orders to take off our ponchos and stow them in our fanny packs. I got mine off and stowed, but the soldier marching in front of me was having trouble getting his poncho into his pack. He whispered and asked me to stuff the poncho into his pack, but as I was attempting to accomplish this feat, a large figure loomed over my right shoulder. It was the senior DI! He looked at me and asked in a booming voice, "Son, what in hell are you doing fiddling with that man's ass?" I had no reply!

My emotional state fluctuated from hopeful and upbeat to near-depression and I worried constantly about the future. Hand-to-hand combat training was exciting and I did well with the moves we were taught. I had never realized that it could be so easy to kill another man, and I hoped that I would never have to put my training into practice. It was a good way to relieve some frustration, and it gave me a great deal of confidence in my own abilities. The rifle range held a special fascination for me because my dad had taught me to hunt and shoot at an early age. I was not surprised when I qualified as an expert with the M-14 rifle one cold, windy day along with three other men from my platoon. As a reward for our shooting prowess we were driven back to the barracks in a Jeep instead of having to make the long march. That award proved to be short-lived, however, because when we got back to the barracks we were promptly sent to the mess hall to report for KP (kitchen police) duty!

Some of the DIs seemed to enjoy taunting the trainees and making their lives as difficult as possible. One DI in particular, even though he was a small man, was especially obnoxious and took great delight in bullying the men. On one occasion, during training with pugil sticks, he proceeded to beat hell out of one of the trainees and boasted that he doubted there was anyone in the company who would "have the balls" to take him on. Just then, a deep voice from the rear said, "I'll try." With that, a very large black trainee stepped forward and took one of the pugil sticks and prepared for a round with the cocky DI. It took no time at all for the black trainee to knock the DI on his back. Then he proceeded to beat and pummel the prone DI with his pugil stick and would likely have severely injured the man, but several other instructors stepped in and restrained the victorious trainee. From then on, the victorious trainee became a legend in the company and the cocky DI became very quiet.

Toward the end of basic training, the whole company got a weekend pass to go to Nashville. We all boarded a bus and headed out the main gate, happy to be away from Fort Campbell if only for a weekend. As soon as we got to the bus terminal in Nashville, everyone seemed to scatter in all directions. Many of the young, single soldiers went looking for women and had no trouble finding them. My bunkmate in Fort Campbell evidently found the wrong woman, because he came back with a case of clap and ended up on sick call for a penicillin shot. He was then put on disciplinary report and did more than his share of KP duty. Another married soldier and I got a hotel room and called home to talk with our wives. We spent our time walking around Nashville, watching TV, and most of all, eating anything that did not resemble army chow. After calling home several times and talking with Linda and my folks, my spirits lifted considerably and I was ready to finish basic and move on to the next phase of my training, regardless of where that might be.

We spent the following week on bivouac in the woods near several rifle ranges we routinely used. The weather was miserable and it snowed on us, then rained. Most of the time was spent on the ranges shooting our M-14s and going through other training exercises. At night we slept in shelter halves (pup tents) wrapped up in our down sleeping bags. It was miserable, but we managed to stay warm and dry most of the time. Our final day was spent learning wilderness survival techniques, and one of the tasks we were given was to kill and cook our own food. The army brought in a truckload of live chickens, which they set loose in an area, and we were supposed to catch, kill, and eat one for supper. It turned out to be a disaster, with few men able to catch the wary chickens and fewer still who had the heart to kill one. After what seemed like an episode from a Three Stooges movie, the chicken-catching exercise was cancelled and we were issued C-rations to eat.

A couple of weeks later we graduated from basic training with very little fanfare and anxiously awaited our orders as we stood in formation on the parade field. Since I was one of several soldiers who had earlier spent a day training to drive large transport trucks, I hoped that I would be assigned to a transportation company. That did not happen. When my name was called, I was assigned to an MOS (Military Occupation Specialty) of 11-B (infantry), as was most of the company. I did not know it then, but found out later, that around 90 percent of all draftees became "11-Bravos" and were assigned to the infantry. Within hours of graduating from basic training we boarded a bus again, this time headed for Fort Polk in southern Louisiana. We had heard all about Fort Polk. It was reputed to be a hell-hole in the swamps of Louisiana, infested with mosquitoes and snakes. It was not what I had hoped for, but then again, nobody asked me.

The bus ride to Fort Polk was interesting to me because I had never seen the South before. We stopped and ate lunch in Memphis and continued south through the farmlands and cotton fields of Mississippi. We ate dinner somewhere in Louisiana, and I got my first taste of Cajun food, which I really enjoyed. The bus arrived at Fort Polk just after midnight, and I noticed a large billboard just inside the gate that welcomed new trainees. It referred to us as "Infantry Replacements for Vietnam." That was a stark reminder that I did not want to see. We arrived at a large reception building and stood around for hours while we waited to be processed. The DIs in charge would not let anyone go to sleep, and I thought that the night would never end. Finally we got finished with the paperwork and were allowed to sleep for about two hours in the transient barracks before we were called into formation and marched over to our new company area. The senior DI was a big, mean, redneck bully who set an early example for all of us by physically assaulting a black recruit who was talking while in formation when he should have been quiet. After that, nobody ever challenged the senior DI or questioned any of his commands. Most of the black recruits hated the senior DI, and the rest of us had no use for him either. Our platoon DI seemed somewhat arrogant at times but he was easy to get along with and he was respected by the men. He was one of very few drill instructors I encountered who did not use profanity. He had just come back from Vietnam after a tour with the 25th Infantry Division, which had been taking heavy casualties between Saigon and the Cambodian border area. He told us that his only objective was to teach us all that he knew so that we would come back from Vietnam alive. I listened to every word he said and, as it turned out, I was damn glad that I did. The learning curve in an infantry unit was steep, and those who did not catch on quickly or take advice often paid a high price.

Unlike during basic training, men were routinely issued weekend passes at Fort Polk as long as they had not screwed up somehow. Most went into either Leesville or DeRidder to drink and party with the local ladies. There was often trouble in town, and several soldiers ended up in jail or were beaten up by local men in the bars. I never had the desire to go into either town, so I spent my weekends going to movies or to the bowling alley with several friends from our training company. One of the big hit movies that kept playing for weeks was *The Green Berets,* starring John Wayne. It drew huge audiences and served as an ideal propaganda film for the army.

Training at Fort Polk seemed to go by fast, and it consisted of a lot of the same things we learned at Fort Campbell, but the instruction was more intense and detailed. Most of the troops seemed to sense that this was more than just harassment and paid close attention, since the one thing you failed to learn might be what got you killed. New things were added to the training, including live night-fire courses and night navigation through swamps that were crawling with alligators and water moccasins. There were more weapons to learn about: claymore mines, different kinds of grenades, and other devices that we would need to know about when we got to Vietnam. We carried M-16 rifles now instead of the old M-14s we carried at Fort Campbell. Everyone learned to field-strip and care for his rifle, and we often spent long hours cleaning and re-cleaning them until both our platoon leader and

DI were satisfied that the rifles were spotless. We continued to practice our marksmanship on the rifle ranges, but now we were taught a new technique called "quick kill." It was a method of instinctive firing at close range and it actually worked. It did not replace marksmanship, but it helped soldiers to react to enemy troops who were often within a few meters in the jungle. All during training a rumor circulated that our class would be sent to Germany.

There was an outbreak of spinal meningitis on the base, and the post surgeon ordered that all troops be trucked rather than marched to the rifle ranges and other training facilities. He also ordered that all troops had to get at least eight hours of sleep every night, which made him a great guy in our eyes. This made physical training fairly easy for most of the 12 weeks at Fort Polk, but toward the end of our training the meningitis outbreak was declared over and the kid-glove treatment ended abruptly. We were marched mercilessly then and had to run for hours. Many men had gotten a little out of shape, and they were dropping like flies on the long runs in the spring heat and humidity.

Our training culminated with a week in the pine-covered hills of Louisiana at a place called Tiger Ridge. It was a realistic exercise, complete with soldiers dressed up as Viet Cong and a model Vietnamese village. We practiced ambush techniques, patrolling, and setting up camps. There were mock prisoner interrogations and instructions about the Geneva Convention. We got the chance to ride in APCs (armored personnel carriers), though few men in Vietnam would ever get that chance. One night while making camp one of the men caught a small, colorful snake and was letting it crawl around on his hand. He told me it was a king snake, but after observing the color pattern and remembering the old saying, "Red and black, friend of Jack, red and yellow, kill a fellow," I informed the man that he was playing with a coral snake. Lucky for him, coral snakes are fairly docile and it did not bite him, but he let it go in a hurry. After a final week on Tiger Ridge playing war games, we were ready to graduate and go home on a 30-day leave. At that time we also found out that the big rumor about Germany was just that. Every soldier in the platoon got after-leave orders to report to Oakland Army Depot, where he would undergo further processing before being transported to the Republic of Vietnam.

After getting over the disappointment of getting orders for Vietnam, my spirits lifted as I packed and prepared to fly to Wisconsin to begin my 30-day leave. During the flight home all I could think about was spending a month with Linda and my family. I wanted to relax, visit all my friends, and make sure that everything was in order for Linda before I left for Vietnam.

The army tried to do a good job of training us physically and teaching us the necessary combat skills. As I would soon learn in Vietnam, the training was not specialized enough and it was not adequate for the situation and the enemy we would encounter. Much of what I and other troops learned about survival in Vietnam was from on-the-job training. The one thing the army did not and could not prepare us for was the mental and emotional stress we were about to experience in Vietnam.

2

Welcome to Vietnam

My 30-day leave in Wisconsin went by way too fast for me, but it was nice while it lasted. I did some fishing and spent time at Lake Emily, where I spent many summers as a boy. Many of my friends stopped to wish me well and we hit most of the watering holes we had frequented during college breaks. My dad and I spent time together fishing and just sitting on the porch. We tried to reassure each other that everything would work out and the next year would go by rapidly. I think we both harbored many lingering doubts, but neither of us expressed those fears. Most of all, I enjoyed spending time with Linda and Tim. We took a trip to northern Wisconsin to visit some of our favorite country and ended up doing a lot of talking about what we planned to do when I got back from Vietnam. Though I was well aware of the dangers and risks that I faced in the year ahead, I was careful to avoid expressing my concerns to Linda. She had enough on her mind already and I did not want to worry her even more.

Halfway through May it was time to rejoin the army and begin my one-year tour of duty in Vietnam. Both Linda and I dreaded this day, but it finally came and it was time to accept reality and deal with it. After a very difficult and tearful goodbye, I hugged Linda and my mother, wondering if I would see them again. My dad and my brother drove me about 30 miles north to the Mosinee Regional Airport, where I was scheduled for a flight to Oakland, California. While we waited in the terminal, my dad was unusually quiet. He said a few things to me, but my mind was so numb I really did not hear him. I talked briefly with my brother James, who was on leave from the U.S. Navy, and all he could think to say was, "Don't get yourself killed." After handshakes and hugs, I boarded the plane for my first flight west from Wisconsin. As the jet rumbled down the runway and picked up speed for takeoff, I choked back a tear, said a prayer and wondered how the year ahead would play itself out. The flight was uneventful and thousands of thoughts raced through my mind. I tried to think about some of the things I had learned in basic and advanced infantry training, but it was difficult for me to focus. I thought mostly about Linda and Tim. I would miss them so much. Three hours later the pilot announced that we would be landing soon at Stapleton International Airport in Denver. It was my first glimpse of Denver and the Rocky Mountains, and I was surprised that the higher peaks were still covered with snow. After a brief stop, the plane flew toward the west coast, and two hours later it touched down at San Francisco International Airport. My sister Barbara and her husband Bill were waiting for me in the terminal, and we headed for San Mateo, where they lived.

I spent the next couple of days visiting with them, enjoying my first glimpse of California, and catching up on the latest news. My brother-in-law was a pilot, and he took me on a flight in a Cessna around the San Francisco Bay for a bird's-eye view of the area. It was very interesting, and I enjoyed my first look at the Golden Gate Bridge, which was shrouded by wisps of fog. My heart was not in it, though, because I had bigger things on my mind. When it was time for me to report for duty, Barb and Bill drove me across the San Mateo Bridge to Oakland and dropped me off at the Oakland Army Depot. I waved goodbye as I grabbed my duffel bag, walked through the gate and showed the guard my orders. I was not certain what to expect next, and my mind began to wander again as I pondered whether I would be coming back this way again alive or in a metal casket.

The Oakland Army Depot was a very busy place, and people were bustling about everywhere I looked. It was surprisingly well organized, and processing did not take too long. After I reported for duty and gave the processing clerk my orders, he sent me to a large warehouse area where men were getting their tropical clothing issue. Most of the clothing that I brought with me in the duffel bag, as I was instructed to do, was collected. The field jacket that I was issued at Fort Campbell was tossed onto a large pile with all the other field jackets that men brought with them. I wanted to keep the jacket and wondered why I had been such a fool to have brought it with me on my way to Vietnam. I was issued new jungle fatigues and jungle boots and got a fresh haircut. Unbelievably, everyone received a couple more immunizations. To help pass the time I went to a movie and afterwards ordered the last hamburger and french fries that I would eat for a while. After that, there was little to do but sit and wait until my name was called and I got put on a flight manifest. Along with hundreds of other men, I sat around for most of the day in a large hangar bay trying to read, sleep or otherwise keep occupied. I struck up a conversation with a guy named Ray, and we exchanged the latest scuttlebutt on Vietnam. After getting a couple hours of sleep on the hangar floor, I went to the restroom, and while I was shaving I dropped my wedding ring in the sink and it disappeared down the drain. My heart sank; the ring was my only connection to my wife and home. I decided that there was no way I was going anywhere without retrieving my ring first, so I found a janitor and told him what had happened. He got a wrench and disconnected the pipe under the sink so I could retrieve my ring. I put it back on and never removed it during my entire tour of duty in Vietnam.

After many boring hours, the flight manifest with my name and more than a hundred other soldiers' names was announced. We grabbed our duffel bags and boarded buses for the short trip to Travis Air Force Base. As soon as we arrived we were ushered into a large mess hall. After we ate a very good dinner that some soldiers jokingly called the "last supper," we boarded a Flying Tigers jet for Vietnam. The most memorable year in my life had just begun. On the long flight to Vietnam I tried to sleep as much as possible, but with all the thoughts racing through my mind, sleep was difficult. The plane made a brief stop in Anchorage to refuel, and I was impressed with the beautiful snow-capped mountains that I saw in the distance. One soldier remarked that he just felt like grabbing his duffel bag and heading for the mountains. Most of us were anxious and talked about our homes and families and what kind of units we were going to be in once we arrived in Vietnam. I was struck by the fact that most of the men were headed to infantry units. It was also evident that nobody was traveling as part of a unit; each of us was alone. We stopped again to refuel in Tokyo, and we were allowed to go into the terminal to buy snacks and souvenirs. The airport was crowded with Japanese people, and it was the first time in my life that I had actually felt like a minority.

Finally, after about 22 hours, the moment of truth came when our pilot announced that we were nearing Bien Hoa Airbase, just northeast of Saigon. He told us that the plane would be in a holding pattern for a while because the base was under a rocket and mortar attack. Everyone craned their necks to look out the windows and see what was going on. I could see red and green tracers floating through the air far below along with occasional flashes, which I assumed were explosions. After about 20 minutes the attack ceased and the plane banked sharply and began a steep approach into Bien Hoa. After we landed without incident, the plane was deadly silent except for soldiers pulling items from the overhead compartments.

Stepping from the air-conditioned plane into the oppressive heat and humidity of night-time Vietnam sucked my breath away. If that wasn't enough, the smell of diesel fuel and other foreign odors that I could not yet identify was nauseating. We quickly proceeded into a large hangar where we collected our duffel bags after a short wait. Then we got a brief "Welcome to Vietnam" speech from some lieutenant who seemed like he was anxious to get back to whatever he had been doing before we arrived. We then boarded buses for a ride to the 90th Replacement Battalion in Long Binh. The windows on the bus were open but covered with wire mesh. I quickly figured out that this was not to keep us inside, but rather to keep thrown objects out. We began the ride just as the morning light was breaking, and the bus made its way through a residential area that was crowded with tin-roofed shanties. It was worse than any slum I had seen and the air was thick with wood smoke and fishy odors. I saw Vietnamese people for the first time, and I was surprised that so many people were up and scurrying about at that hour of the morning, especially the small children. There were *lambrettas* (small motorbikes) and other vehicles everywhere. The streets were lined with small shops containing many items for sale including chickens in cages, fruits, and vegetables. The older men and women were dressed in black or white shirts and pants and wore conical straw hats. Many of the older women carried bundles or jugs balanced on the ends of six-foot poles. Younger women wore colorful dresses called *ao dais* over white slacks. Some of the younger children waved and shouted at us in broken English. Many approached the bus holding out their hands,

Map of South Vietnam, 1969-70.

begging for food, yelling, "You gimme chop chop." The adults simply stared at us as if they wondered who we were and what we wanted in their country.

After a short ride we arrived at the 90th Replacement Battalion and were ushered into a mess hall and fed our first meal in Vietnam. It was actually pretty good and consisted of eggs, bacon, fruit, juice, toast, and coffee. After finishing breakfast, we were assigned to barracks to wait for instructions on further processing and assignments to our new units. The barracks, or hootches as they were called in Vietnam, were basically plywood-sided structures with large screens for windows and air circulation. The roofs were made of corrugated metal, and every hootch had a wall of sandbags about 5 feet high piled around it. Someone had posted a small sign beside the entrance to our hootch that read: "Welcome to Vietnam! You will see strange sights, meet strange people, and kill them!"

I met a number of guys, most of whom I never saw again. There was a good cross-section of soldiers from all over, but I especially remember a group of guys from Hawaii who kept everyone in good spirits by telling jokes. We spent most of the day filling sandbags, and I was surprised that nobody seemed to harass us like they did during basic training. The heat and humidity sapped my appetite and strength and I could not eat much. I was constantly thirsty and drank a lot of lukewarm, chlorinated water even though it had an awful taste.

That night I went to the EM (enlisted men's) club, and after a few beers I ran into a soldier who was from my hometown. Don had been in Vietnam for a year and was on his way back home. We talked for at least two hours, and I listened intently to everything he said. Don had been assigned to the 101st Airborne Division as a forward artillery observer, and he related one tale after another about his tour of duty. His unit had operated mostly in the Ashau Valley just east of the Laotian border. They had been mortared several times and had been in numerous firefights. He had also been on Firebase Airborne when it was overrun by a large NVA (North Vietnamese Army) unit. (A detailed account of the battle for Firebase Airborne can be found in the book *Hamburger Hill* by Samuel Zaffiri.) Don's parting advice to me was, "Whatever you do, don't get yourself assigned to the 101st Airborne Division. Some really bad shit happens in the Ashau!"

Because of the heat and the wild thoughts that kept racing through

Author after arrival at Bien Hoa.

my mind, I had a hard time getting any sleep after talking with Don, and I laid in my bunk with sweat soaking my entire body. After what seemed like hours, I finally drifted off into an uneasy sleep but was awakened abruptly by several loud explosions and the sound of wailing sirens. There were several very loud "ka-booms" followed by more explosions that sounded different to me. Everyone hit the cement floor and began to low-crawl to the sandbagged bunker that stood just outside the door. Other than some skinned knees and elbows, everyone seemed to be unhurt as we huddled inside the bunker. After a few more loud explosions, things seemed to quiet down and we waited nervously until a young second lieutenant approached and told us that some rockets and mortar rounds had hit the nearby airport runway. He told us to return to our hootches and get some sleep. With all the chatter that was occurring among a bunch of very nervous soldiers who had just arrived in Vietnam, nobody got much sleep the rest of the night. Finally, it hit me. I was actually in Vietnam!

The next day ended up being another long day on sandbag detail, which seemed to be the thing to do in Vietnam whenever any spare time was available. The area selected for filling sandbags was almost always in the most shade-free spot that could be found! Though it was a boring job, it gave me the opportunity to talk with other soldiers and catch up on the latest rumors — which usually turned out to be false. Later, on several occasions during my tour in Vietnam, I was very thankful to have a row of sandbags between me and incoming mortar rounds. After a few hours of filling sandbags and sweating, the guys from Hawaii declared that the day was over, threw down their shovels, and left. Nobody seemed to care what we did, so a few minutes later the rest of us knocked off and headed for the EM club, where we spent the rest of the day drinking beer and sitting under the large overhead fans trying to keep cool.

Several of us were assigned to bunker guard for that night and reported for duty just after we ate evening chow. We were briefed by the OIC (officer-in-charge) of the bunker line, and four men were assigned to each bunker on the perimeter of the base. The bunkers were large structures built with heavy timbers and covered with several layers of sandbags. There were several firing ports in front and a covered crow's-nest on top for observation. The bunkers were spaced about 40 meters apart and several rows of concertina wire were strung in front of them. We were issued M-16 rifles, fragmentation grenades, and starlight scopes which allowed us to see in the dark. We got instructions regarding procedures for detonating claymore mines and the 55-gallon fougasse drums, which were located in the concertina wire in front of the bunkers. This was the first time I had seen fougasse drums, which contained jellied gasoline similar to napalm. These drums could be detonated and the flaming fougasse would cover enemy infiltrators, burning them alive. That night was my first on guard duty in Vietnam, and not knowing just what to expect, I spent it sitting in silence watching the night skies and straining my eyes to see if any VC (Viet Cong) were sneaking up on the bunker. Occasionally, I saw tracers that floated through the thick air somewhere beyond our perimeter and I wondered if some unit was in a firefight. During my turn on guard I scanned the wire in front of the bunker with a starlight scope, expecting to see gooks coming through the wire at any minute. I saw nothing. Luckily, the night passed quietly, and I was glad to see daylight approach. The OIC came around in a Jeep, collected our gear, and released us from guard duty. I was finally starting to get my appetite back, so I headed for the mess hall to get some powdered eggs and greasy sausage for breakfast.

Right after breakfast we were all assembled again in front of the orderly room to see if this would be the day that we got assigned to our units. After the usual wait, the names were called out and assignments were made. Several men were assigned to a transportation unit near Saigon, and a couple of guys I had met on sandbag detail got assigned to helicopter units. Most of the men, however, were getting assigned to various infantry units located all over Vietnam. I was hoping to get assigned to the 25th Infantry Division because my DI at Fort Polk had served with the 25th and had given the division high marks for its effectiveness. Finally, the officer making the assignments called my name. I'll never forget what he said. "Nesser, 101st Airborne Division, 2nd Battalion, 501st Infantry." Shit! I couldn't believe it! I realized that my worst fears had come to pass. As I stood there with several other soldiers who had also been assigned to the 101st, a group of veterans who were processing out and heading home walked by and said, "Good luck, you poor bastards." We had all heard about the battle for Dong Ap Bia, better known as Hamburger Hill, which had just taken place in the Ashau Valley. We realized that we were fresh meat replacing the casualties from that battle. Those of us going to the 101st were told to get our gear and report for transportation to SERTS (Screaming Eagles Replacement Training School). The week-long training was mandatory for all incoming troops and was designed to introduce replacements to the rigors of combat in Vietnam and to acclimatize them to the hot, humid weather.

The week at SERTS was spent going over everything we had learned at Fort Polk but with much more intensity. The instructors were all combat veterans and they were exceptional. Most of us realized that this was for real, not some basic training bullshit, and we listened to every word uttered by our instructors. There was live night-fire training, and I could swear that the M-60 machine gun tracer rounds were only six inches above my head. We were told that a man in the previous training class had panicked and stood up during the night-fire exercise. Supposedly he was hit with machine-gun fire and had died, though most of us suspected that it never happened and was a story. While we were crawling through the mud in an obstacle course, the instructors set off explosive devices that were planted in various locations along the course. These explosions were meant to simulate grenades or mortar fire, presumably, and the first time one went off near me, it scared the crap out of me. The blast was not big but it did blow wet mud high into the air. When the mud rained down and landed on my back, it felt like somebody had beaned me with a baseball. We learned various techniques for setting ambushes, the correct way to set up an NDP (night defensive position), how to fire a weapon in the dark, and how to avoid booby traps. Learning the proper techniques for scanning terrain for movement and objects that were out of place proved to be invaluable when I had to walk point later in my tour. The proper method for seeing in the dark was also something that was essential. The skills we were taught were valuable and I suspect that many men came home alive because they paid attention and learned what they needed to survive. However, I learned other things very soon. Many survival skills were not taught during training and had to be learned quickly if one's chances for survival were to be increased. Sometimes, however, all the skills in the world could not save you if you happened to be in the wrong place at the wrong time. Even the best soldiers were wounded or killed.

When the intense week of training was over, we boarded a C-130 cargo plane for a flight to I Corps (the northernmost military province in South Vietnam) where we would be assigned and transported to our field units. The plane seemed like a bucket of bolts as it lumbered down the runway at Bien Hoa and lifted off for our flight north. It vibrated badly and was so loud that conversation was impossible. During the flight a thousand thoughts raced through my mind, but my main concern was whether the tin can we were flying in would hold together until we reached our destination! After about two hours the big C-130 circled and landed at the airport in Phu Bai. The company clerk was waiting in a Jeep and we drove to Camp Sally, where the 2nd Battalion, 501st Infantry was head-quartered.

3

The Ashau Valley

Camp Sally was located just northwest of the ancient imperial capital city of Hue on flat sandy coastal lowlands near foothills that gave rise to the Annamese Cordillera a few miles to the west. The mountains were steep and covered with a carpet of green jungle vegetation. They were often shrouded in mist, which gave them an eerie, forboding appearance. Sally was a sprawling camp with seemingly endless rows of metal-roofed hootches and various other administrative and supply buildings and tents. Everything in the camp was coated with yellowish sandy dirt because of the dust created by the constant movement of helicopters, trucks, and jeeps. Men were bustling about doing their jobs and helicopters were constantly departing for and returning from points unknown to me at the time. I was taken to the Alpha Company orderly room, and the company clerk had me fill out more paperwork. Then I was sent to the company supply hootch to get all of the equipment that I would need for the field. I also learned that I would be joining Alpha Company the following morning but that they were not at Camp Sally; they were currently operating somewhere in the Ashau Valley.

After I picked up all my gear, I sat on my cot in the hootch that I was assigned to for the night and stared at the mountain of gear, trying to figure out just where to start. I was pretty overwhelmed and had no real idea of how I was going to stuff all of that crap into one damn rucksack. Several veterans who were back at Camp Sally to begin their R&R leave watched with amusement as I tried to act like I knew what I was doing but could not seem to get everything to fit in my rucksack. Finally one guy who must have felt sorry for me came over and said, "Here, let me show you how to stow all this shit." I was inwardly grateful and watched with some amazement as he started to fit everything into place. In short order, there it was. A completely packed rucksack, ready for action! Somehow, the following gear had been packed inside the rucksack or attached to it: 18 clips of M-16 ammo, six HE (high explosive) rounds for the squad's M-79 grenade launcher, two trip flares, a one-pound block of C4 plastic explosive, 300 rounds of ammo for the squad's M-60 machine gun, two smoke grenades, one claymore mine, four frags (fragmentation grenades), an entrenching tool, a machete, six one-quart canteens, 12 C-ration meals (at first I was not smart enough to take them out of the box so they would fit in my rucksack until the veteran showed me how to break them down), a poncho and poncho liner, four compress bandages, heat tabs, iodine tabs, insect repellent, a towel, extra socks, personal toiletries, writing materials, my buck knife, and my cigarettes and lighter.

Author in combat gear before mission.

The helmet or steel pot that we were issued provided some protection from shrapnel and bullets and was often used as a wash basin for shaving. Valuables such as wallets, letters, cigarettes and matches could be tucked inside between the webbing and the helmet for protection from the frequent downpours that were so common in Vietnam. The helmets were heavy and hot, but our unit required us to wear them except for night ambushes, when we often wore floppy jungle hats which would not make noise if they were accidentally dropped. While some units in Vietnam wore flak jackets, our unit did not wear them in the field because they were considered too heavy and too hot to be practical. As the supply sergeant said, "Hell, if we wore them damn things half the men in the company would be dying from heat stroke." I carried the standard M-16 assault rifle, which fired a 5.56mm bullet with an effective range of just over 400 meters.

Although many of the earlier-model M-16s apparently jammed frequently, they were replaced with newer, redesigned M-16s by the time I got to Vietnam. These rifles were more reliable than the older version and mine never jammed. We kept them as clean as we could, and I believe that they were a far more rugged weapon than many people thought. Our clips held 20 rounds, though we never loaded them with more than 18 rounds in order to prevent jamming. After a few months in the field, I traded in my M-16 and carried an M-79 grenade launcher, often called either a thumper or a blooper because of the sound it made when it was fired. It broke open like a sawed-off single-barrel shotgun and held one 40mm round, usually an HE (high explosive) round with an effective range of about 400 meters. The HE round armed itself by centrifugal force after it was fired and had to travel about 20 meters before it would explode. This was to prevent it from exploding too close to the grenadier or other soldiers. When the round struck its intended target, it had a casualty radius of about five meters. The weapon would also fire illumination rounds and shotgun rounds which were like a large shotgun shell loaded with buckshot. Shotgun rounds were particularly effective when walking point, although you had only one shot and could not afford to miss.

In order to pick up the loaded rucksack I had to sit and get the straps over my shoulders, then rock forward to get up. The damn thing seemed to weigh a ton, though actually most of the loaded rucks weighed somewhere between 60 and 80 pounds, depending on the mission. I was just thankful that I did not have to tote an M-60 machine gun. They weighed 23 pounds and were awkward to carry but could fire 600 rounds a minute. I had great respect for machine gunners because their job was not easy. Not only did the weight of the weapon kick his butt, a machine gunner was usually a prime target for the enemy.

I stowed my gear and went to get some chow, which was quite inferior to the chow we were served at the 90th Replacement Battalion. At least I was regaining my appetite, and as it turned out, I would need all the strength I could muster in the field. I wondered how I was going to be able to walk with that heavy ruck on my back, but some old-timers assured me that I would get used to it quickly or would die of exhaustion from trying. That thought certainly did not help to buoy my spirits. Luckily, I was not assigned to bunker guard duty, so I went back to my hootch and wrote letters to Linda and my parents, then turned in for the night. I could not sleep as my mind concocted various scenarios of what might happen in the morning, and I was apprehensive about joining the men who would be my comrades for the next year.

I got up at 0500 hours and went to the mess tent, where I ate a quick breakfast of powdered eggs, greasy sausages, toast and coffee. I did not know anyone in the mess tent, so I sat by myself, alone with my thoughts. After breakfast I went back to the hootch and managed to get saddled up with my rucksack and head to the helipad with three other cherries (fresh, inexperienced troops) who were also headed to the field to join Alpha Company. I soon learned that everyone referred to the field as the "boonies" or "bush." The early morning sky was beautiful and the air seemed cool, but as soon as the sun got up in the sky, it began to get hot and steamy. Sweat poured off of my head, steaming up my glasses. My jungle fatigues were soaked and flies buzzed around as we waited for our flight out to the boonies. About 0800 hours, a Huey helicopter landed on the helipad and the door gunner motioned for us to board. This was all new to me and I barely got my butt into the Huey before it took off and hovered briefly, then dropped its nose and sped off. My feet were hanging out of the open-sided aircraft and the door gunner could see that I was a cherry who was new to the routine. I was worried and tried to grab on to anything that I could to keep from falling out. The gunner yelled at me over the "whop-

whop-whop" noise of the rotor, "Don't worry, you ain't gonna fall out." As I learned later, the centrifugal force kept us inside, and after a few flights I began to enjoy flying. The views were always pretty good, the air was usually much cooler than on the ground, and the adrenaline rush felt intense.

The Huey circled Camp Sally and headed west toward a distant chain of mountains which looked purple and hazy in the morning light. The air felt cool, which was a welcome relief, and I watched green rice fields and small villages pass by below. I could see farmers in the fields with their water buffalo and people moving about in the villages. For a few moments, at least, I was enjoying these new sights and my mind was focused on something other than the war. In about 20 minutes the Huey was over the foothills and getting closer to the looming mountains, which were covered with a beautiful green carpet of jungle. A winding river that I later learned was the Song Bo (Perfume River) snaked along through the valley far below us. I was enjoying my first bird's-eye view of the landscape that was to be my home for more than a year, and it was hard to imagine that this idyllic-looking country was so troubled by war. After about a half-hour of flying, the Huey descended abruptly and touched down on the helipad at Firebase Currahee. We were practically shoved off the helicopter, and as soon as we got off, six other troops waiting on the pad quickly boarded. The chopper took off and headed back toward Camp Sally and relative civilization. All four of us reported to the company HQ (headquarters) bunker and were told where to stow our gear and to report for a detail filling sandbags. If there was one job that was ubiquitous in Vietnam, it was filling sandbags. The burning sun beat down as we spent all day filling one sandbag after another and piling them to reinforce a bunker on the perimeter of the firebase. Firebase Currahee was a chaotic-looking collection of bunkers and howitzers surrounded by row after row of concertina wire. It sat on a relatively flat valley floor surrounded by steep, ominous-looking mountains which were covered with triple-canopy jungle. I could hardly believe that I was in the middle of the Ashau Valley, one of the most dangerous places in Vietnam.

After eating a quick supper of C-rations, nobody really told me or the other new troops anything so all four of us decided to spend the night near a pile of culverts just inside the bunker line. The day had really tired me out, and I drifted off into an uneasy sleep but was abruptly awakened about 0300 hours when all hell broke loose. Weapons were firing all around the perimeter, and I could see red tracers flying out from the firebase as I hunkered down low and strained my eyes to see what the hell was going on. Just as abruptly as it had started, the firing ceased and all was quiet. In a minute or so a soldier who turned out to be the officer in charge of the bunker line approached our position. We asked what was going on, and he just replied "mad minute" and left. I later learned that this was a common practice on firebases. At a predetermined time of the night or early morning, the bunker line would open fire into the concertina wire and area surrounding the base on the chance that they might catch enemy sappers (elite NVA commandos) trying to infiltrate the base. The rest of the night passed without further incident, but nobody seemed to be able to sleep and several of us laid there whispering to each other and trying to keep the swarms of mosquitoes away from us without much luck.

After checking again with HQ the next morning, we were told grab our gear and head for the helipad to board a log bird (supply helicopter) that was headed out to resupply Alpha Company with food and ammo. We all waited nervously next to the pad, and about 0730 hours a Huey touched down and we jumped aboard with our gear. It was a rather short flight to a small LZ (landing zone) in the jungle where Alpha Company was waiting for resupply and getting ready to move out for the day. The LZ was a recently cleared opening in the jungle that was just large enough to allow the Huey to touch down safely. Again, we were literally pushed out of the chopper as soon as the skids touched the ground. The resupply was kicked out right behind us. We crouched and then headed for a guy who was waving us over as other troops ran out and picked up the ammo and C-rations that had just been delivered. The man waving us over was the company first sergeant, who quickly assigned two soldiers to the 2nd Platoon. The other man and I were assigned to the 1st Platoon, but before any of us went over to join our platoons, the CO (commanding officer) walked over toward us to brief us on the company's location and gave us some other general information related to our mission. I began to salute him but was quickly told, "Don't ever salute me!" I learned that unlike the stateside custom, officers in the field were not saluted. I also noticed that they wore subdued or no insignia at all. This was to keep them

River somewhere near the Ashau Valley.

from being identified by enemy snipers and shot. Since they were usually near the RTO and radio, they were a target anyway. The CO was a captain, about 35 years old, and he tried to put us at ease. We learned that we were somewhere near the Laotian border close to the Ho Chi Minh Trail, and our mission was to patrol and try to make contact with the NVA unit that was reported to be in the area. He let us know that the NVA was not a rag-tag outfit; they were well-trained soldiers who had good equipment. The only thing they lacked was air power, but their knowledge of the terrain and their tenacity more than made up for that. The CO told us to pay attention to orders and to listen to our squad leaders if we wanted to stay alive very long in Vietnam.

We were led over to join our platoons, and I met our platoon leader who was a young first lieutenant from California whom everyone called L-T (El-Tee, for lieutenant). He was very friendly and I immediately liked him. I also had the impression that he had his head on straight and knew what he was doing. My squad leader, a tall guy named Rich, was a veteran of the Hamburger Hill battle. Other troops told me that he "had his

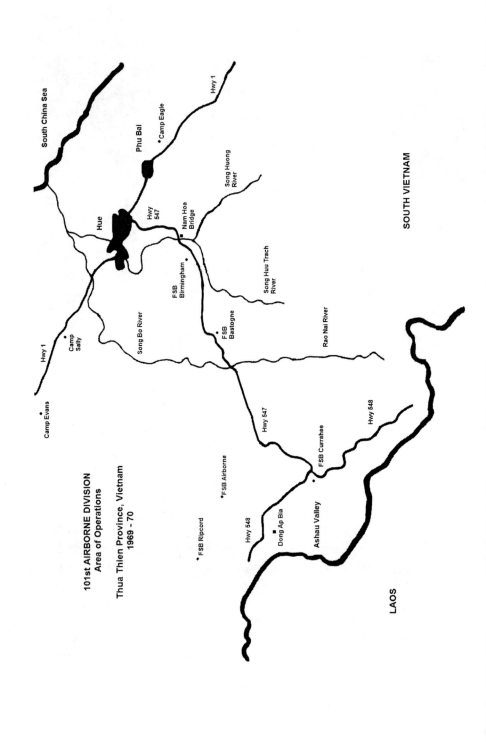

101st AIRBORNE DIVISION
Area of Operations

Thua Thien Province, Vietnam
1969 - 70

shit together," but he also seemed very edgy. I watched intently and observed how the other men in the platoon rolled up ponchos and other gear and packed up their rucksacks for the day's movement through the jungle. It was fairly quiet and most of the men looked tired and worn out, but there was also a definite look of alertness on their faces. I took my cue from that look and after some brief small talk, the company was ready to move out.

I was in the middle of the squad column as we moved out and slowly made our way along a steep jungle trail that wound along a mountainside. The trail was a narrow dirt path with rocks poking out every few feet, and walking was not easy. The jungle was so thick that visibility was very limited, and I kept wondering how in hell we would be able to see the enemy. The heat was oppressive and the vegetation had a dank smell that I will never forget. Hordes of mosquitoes buzzed around my head constantly, and even the foul-smelling army-issued insect repellent did not seem to help very much. Sweat poured off my head and dripped onto my glasses, making them next to useless, and I had to keep wiping them on my dirty jungle fatigues. Our mode of operation was to move slowly for about 20 minutes, then the column would halt for a few minutes. I tried to keep a sharp eye out even though our squad was near the middle of the company-sized patrol, and after a few hours in the jungle heat I felt like I was dying. My shoulders ached from the heavy rucksack digging into my flesh, and when we moved up a steep hill my lungs hurt as I tried to suck in the steamy hot air. It was probably one of the most physically demanding days of my life, and my mind kept telling me "You ain't gonna make it out of this green hell." I wanted to give up several times, but then another voice took over and said "Where the hell do you think you are going to go, stupid? Suck it up and get your ass moving." Some time during the afternoon I felt faint and the trees started to spin. The next thing I knew I was sitting with my rucksack off and the medic, whom everyone just called "Doc," was dribbling water over my face and giving me some salt tablets. He told me that I had passed out from heat exhaustion but would get used to it in a few days. Meanwhile, the machine gunner and his assistant took

Opposite: **Map of 101st Airborne Division Area of Operations, Thua Thien Province, 1969-70.**

the 300 rounds of M-60 ammo from my rucksack since they were low on ammo anyway. The loss of that weight seemed to help me tremendously, if only psychologically. After that incident, which left me shaken and embarrassed, I never passed out again, though I suspect that I came close on a number of occasions. The rest of the day went by very slowly for me. We continued to move for about 20 minutes, then stop. During one halt as everyone sat around smoking or talking in hushed tones, I had to answer nature's call and stepped off into the trees behind some bushes. As I started to move back toward the other men, I soon found myself face to face with the business end of an M-60 machine gun and stopped dead in my tracks. The gunner, a black guy named Marvin, luckily recognized me, and he proceeded to chew my ass.

"If you ever have to make a latrine call again you damn sure better let your buddies know where you're going so they don't mistake you for a gook trying to sneak up on the column. You pull that shit again, troop, and you might get your ass blown away!" I felt really foolish, but the incident drove home a valuable lesson on the importance of letting other men know what was happening.

Even though the day turned out to be a really tough one for me, I still enjoyed the jungle sounds and the beautiful green jungle foliage. I thought about how I had played Tarzan with my brother when I was a boy and how I had dreamed about going to the jungle in Africa someday. Here I was, actually in the jungle! It was not Africa, but it would have to do! We finally halted late in the day to set up for the night, and everyone went to work with his entrenching tool, digging foxholes in predetermined spots around our NDP (night defensive position). The soil was reddish clay and tough to dig in, but we did manage to dig a hole about four feet wide and four feet deep for our four-man fighting position. After we laid out our fields of fire and set up the claymores, we sat down and had C-rations for dinner. I was hungry and the food tasted pretty good. Several guys traded various rations, and I found out that some meal items were more valuable than others. Peaches and pound cake was at the top of just about everyone's list, including mine. Other items that most of us liked were spaghetti and meatballs, beans with franks, boned chicken, ham loaf, turkey loaf, and fruitcake. Almost nobody liked ham and lima beans or scrambled eggs and ham, but just about anything tasted good when you were hungry. Besides the main entree item, there was a B-2 unit that contained crackers and cheese and a B-3 unit of fruit. Each C-ration box also contained a small package of assorted items including matches, a plastic spoon, four cigarettes, toilet paper, instant coffee, and hot chocolate. Everyone acquired a P-38, which was a tiny can opener. They became good-luck charms for many of the men, and I carried the same one during the entire time I was in Vietnam. Now and then we got a special purpose (SP) package from the Red Cross. These large cardboard boxes contained soap, razors, toothbrushes, toothpaste, cigarettes, candy, gum, chewing tobacco, and a few novels. When we could, we often used small pieces of C4 explosive to heat our C-rations and water. This material burned very hot and heated things quickly.

Here I was, getting ready to spend my first real night out in the bush with a bunch of men I barely knew. Somehow, I felt that I was close to them, although for a while most of them gave me and the other cherries a wide berth. Since they did not know us, they did not want to take a chance on being too close to somebody who might do something stupid and get them killed. We were all in a tough situation together and, like it or not, we eventually had to rely completely on one another. Earning the trust of the other guys was very important.

After we finished eating our evening meal of cold C-rations and were sitting around having our last smoke before dark, I heard a low rumbling sound and the ground began to shake. At first I wondered what was happening and began to think it was an earthquake. I must have had a puzzled or worried look on my face, because Rich came over and said, "Relax, it's just an Arc Light mission." He told me that an Arc Light mission was a B-52 air strike and that the Ho Chi Minh Trail, which was close to our current position, was bombed almost every day. During the day we had passed numerous large craters, some filled with water. Now I knew what had made the craters and I could only imagine the awesome power unleashed by the bombs that our B-52s dropped.

The late afternoon light faded quickly and the jungle sounds took over. The night rapidly became pitch black, and I could hardly see my hand in front of my face. Just behind our foxhole we had pitched a low tent made of a poncho stretched between some brush. It was only about 16 inches high, with just enough room so that three men could crawl under it to sleep while the other man knelt in the foxhole on guard. We rotated guard duty every two hours, and when my turn came I felt a mixture of fear and excitement. I crawled out from under the poncho where I had been trying to sleep and carefully knelt in the foxhole. The man that I replaced made sure that he told me where the clacker device that would set off the claymore mine was located. I carefully felt along the edge of the foxhole and found the clacker. Then I hunkered down to watch and listen. It was too dark to see anything, so all I could do was listen for movement. All I could really hear, however, was the constant chirping, buzzing and hoots from insects and other jungle denizens. My mind played tricks on me, and I woke the others several times to say that I thought that I had heard movement to our front. After listening briefly, the veterans assured me that there was nothing out there and they went back to sleep. A million thoughts flashed through my mind as I listened to the jungle sounds and tried in vain to keep the mosquitoes away from my face. The situation seemed almost hopeless as I contemplated the year ahead of me, and I wondered if I would ever make it back to Wisconsin. When it was the next man's turn to stand watch, I was so nervous and excited that I knew I would not be able to sleep. I told the man to sleep; I would stand his watch too since it was the last one before morning. Thankfully, after what seemed like an eternity, the darkness began to fade and my first night in the jungle finally ended without incident. To this day, I still remember that interminably long night and the sounds that I heard. After we had eaten our C-rations for breakfast, we tossed the empty cans into the foxholes and covered everything up with dirt. In about five minutes everyone was rucked up and ready to head down the trail again.

The next five days were almost identical to the first. I was still very nervous and scared that at any minute we would walk into an ambush. Mostly, however, I was bored with the monotony of moving slowly and stopping, over and over. I could tell that I was getting a little more in shape or at least was able to hold up under the weight of my rucksack. I also started to get acclimatized and began to learn how to manage my water intake in the heat and humidity. Restraint had to be used because water was often scarce and one could not simply drink until his thirst was quenched. The mosquitoes and leeches were always present, and it became apparent that they would be a part of my life in the bush. I also noticed that there were areas where all the trees were dead or dying. As I would find out later, Agent Orange was used in many areas in Vietnam. We had heard a lot about booby traps during our training at Fort Campbell and at Fort Polk, so I was expecting that we would be running into them constantly. I asked Rich about booby traps and he told me that the NVA troops used the same trails that we did. Since most of them had just come south from North Vietnam and were not familiar with the terrain, they did not usually set booby traps because their own men would walk into them. We ran into very few booby traps in the mountains; most were set on rice paddy dikes and near more populated areas by local Viet Cong soldiers.

I slowly began to get more acquainted with the men in my squad as we exchanged small talk and traded C-rations and cigarettes. Other than our platoon leader, I was the only man in the platoon who had graduated from college. Because of that and my dark-rimmed glasses, some of the guys called me "Professor." Like most infantry grunts in Vietnam, the men in Alpha Company had a fatalistic philosophy or at least talked as if they did. If they were worried about being wounded or killed, they did not show it. Most of them would simply declare that "When your time is up, it's up!" Another popular phrase, used in association with any bad or undesirable news or event, was "Fuck it, don't mean nothing!"

On the morning of the fifth day we had just moved out and headed down a narrow trail in some very thick jungle when our point man opened up and emptied his M-16. Everyone hit the ground, but after the burst from the point man, no further shots were fired. L-T went running forward to see what had caused the point man to fire his weapon, and after some discussion he came back and told us that as the point man rounded a small bend in the trail he almost ran into an NVA trailwatcher who took off down the trail and disappeared. The point man, who was fairly new in the platoon, had been so excited that his shots just clipped branches about ten feet above his head. The trailwatcher had escaped unharmed and we never saw him again. The poor guy who had been walking point became the object of many jokes about his shooting skills.

Other than the NVA trailwatcher that our point man had surprised, we did not encounter any NVA troops, but we did run across signs indicating that they were there. Rich told me that he thought there was probably an NVA company operating in the area. Nobody said anything, but

I suspect that most of the men were as happy as I was that we did not run into an ambush or end up in a firefight. Since I was new and didn't know much about how the company operated, I had no idea how long we would be stuck out in the bush. I did hear several guys talking and they said that we would be extracted soon. I hoped that they were right.

On the morning of the sixth day the RTO (radio man) got word on the radio that we were going to be extracted by a flight of Hueys and taken to a new AO (area of operations). We began working to clear a small LZ in the jungle, using our machetes to chop down brush and small trees while several men used C4 explosives and detcord (detonation fuse) to blow down larger trees. A large tree was rigged with three bricks of C4 explosive on one side with a one-brick kicker charge on the other, all wrapped with detcord. When it was lit someone yelled, "Fire in the hole" three times just before the charge was detonated and blew the tree down. It took us about three hours to clear the LZ and make it large enough for the Hueys to get in and land to extract us from the area. As soon as the RTO heard on the radio that the choppers were inbound to make the pickup, smoke grenades were popped to mark our location for the pilots. The sight of the Hueys coming in for the extraction looked really great; we were all anxious to get out of the Ashau Valley area. As we lifted off the Hueys picked up speed and headed east. The cool air felt wonderful as it rushed by and I watched the rugged jungle terrain disappear in the distance. In about 30 minutes we reached the foothills and then the rice fields and civilization near Camp Sally. We did not land at Camp Sally, however, and for a while we all thought we were headed to another LZ somewhere in the jungle south toward Da Nang, but the Hueys kept heading farther east toward the coast. Pretty soon I saw the South China Sea just ahead and some of the guys started to smile and do high-fives as they realized that we were going to Eagle Beach. About 10 minutes later we touched down and everyone jumped off the Hueys and headed toward a small building. Eagle Beach was a 101st Airborne in-country R&R center, and other than the familiar metal-roofed barracks, the area looked like a resort anywhere. Palm trees swayed in the gentle sea breeze and I could see men laying on the white sand beach, playing volleyball or swimming in the azure-blue water. It seemed like we had died and gone to heaven.

We spent the next two days relaxing and writing letters. The beach was great and after a game or two of volleyball, most of us went swimming. As I bobbed in the warm water it was hard to realize that I was in Vietnam. At night there was a movie and after that most of us headed for a large EM club, where we could get hamburgers and hot dogs in addition to plenty of cold soda and beer. There was even a massage parlor and barber shop run by local Vietnamese, where most of the guys got a haircut, shave, and a rubdown. Being on a military compound, it was a legitimate establishment, not like the raunchy massage parlors that could be found in Saigon. I got the opportunity to visit and learn more about the men who were in Alpha Company and picked up some good advice on how to stay alive. Noise and light discipline at night was really emphasized. My mind worked overtime trying to remember and process everything I heard. There was so much. How would I remember it all?

I found out that many of these men had been on Firebase Airborne in the Ashau Valley when it was overrun on May 14 by NVA sappers. Though the NVA had been repelled and suffered heavy casualties, 26 Americans had also been killed. A short time later many of these same men were part of the assault on Dong Ap Bia (Hamburger Hill). I was fortunate in many ways to have been assigned to such an experienced unit. That stroke of fate probably gave me the training and the edge I needed to survive. I never got to know most of those men very well and only knew a few of their names. Most of them had been in Vietnam for almost a year and rotated back home soon after I arrived. After the short stay at Eagle Beach, my spirits rose, though the day that I would leave Vietnam seemed very far off. And I wondered if it would ever come.

4

The Jungle

After our brief R&R at Eagle Beach, we began a series of missions in which we were airlifted and inserted into many different LZs throughout our AO (area of operations). Most of the time we were conducting search and destroy missions in the area between the city of Hue and the Ashau Valley. After a while they all seemed to be the same and one mission blended into the next. Several small incidents occurred, but we rarely made contact with the enemy. The NVA were very elusive and obviously did not want to engage us in battle at that time. We were operating mostly in platoon-size elements, and the hot, humid days were endless and boring. After moving anywhere from two to four klicks (kilometers) per day through the jungle, our fatigues were soaked with sweat and we were dog tired. Our usual mode of operation was to stop to eat supper before dark, then move another 300 to 500 meters after it got dark. If enemy scouts were watching they would not know exactly where we were setting up our NDP. After we set up, we often sent out three- or four-man ambush squads to cover a junction in a trail or other likely avenue of enemy approach. The ambush squads set out claymore mines, then hid in deep cover and waited for movement. More often than not, nothing happened. During these ambush missions men often took turns sleeping, but at least one or two remained on alert at all times. Nobody ever got more than three or four hours of sleep at night, and after a while everyone seemed to get used to that routine. I dreaded the long, dark nights because of the mosquitoes and the uncertainty of what might happen. Most of all I hated being alone with my thoughts about contacting the enemy and my worry about Linda and Tim.

View from UH-1 Huey over mountains west of Hue.

One mission had us operating along the Song Bo looking for supply runners along the trails and for cargo moving down the river in sampans. The company split up and each platoon was given a sector of the AO to patrol and observe. The 1st Platoon was assigned to an area just north of the river near several high, rocky ridges. We patrolled a couple of trails that ran parallel to the river, but we did not see anyone else or find any evidence that the NVA were operating in the area. The second or third afternoon, L-T decided to send our squad up to the top of a ridge that would give us a perfect view of the river. We were to set up an observation post when we reached the top and send our SITREPS (situation reports) back every couple of hours. L-T set up his command post close to the river with the other three squads; they would intercept any suspicious river traffic that we reported. It took our squad about two hours to reach the top of the ridge even though it was not high. The going was rough because the slope was very steep and the cover was dense. We had to cut our way through the underbrush with machetes toward the top and hang onto branches to keep from sliding down the slope.

Author prepared for ambush patrol west of Firebase Bastogne.

Once we reached the top the brush thinned out and we found a good spot from which we had a clear view of the river, both upstream and down. Two men began to observe the river while the rest of us began digging in for the night. We felt very safe there because we were hidden from view and there were no trails or paths leading to our position. Just after we had finished eating supper one of the men pointed excitedly up the river. We all crawled over to our observation point and saw a sampan coming down the river. An older man was steering the boat, but we did not see anyone else. We radioed L-T and reported the sampan, then watched as it drew closer. With a few minutes it was almost directly across from us and we heard a shot, then saw the sampan turn and head toward the bank of the river. It stopped near the bank and we saw the 2nd squad board the boat

Sampan on Song Bo River.

to search it. The old man was babbling incoherently and was obviously scared by all the troops on his boat. After a few minutes they got off the boat and L-T motioned for him to continue his journey toward Hue. That night was a good one because we felt relatively safe on the ridge and we all slept well. The next morning we made our way back down the hill and joined the rest of the platoon. L-T told us that the old man had been scared out of his wits and that all he had in the boat was some firewood and a few fish. That day we moved west along the river toward the Ashau Valley.

A few nights later after we finished our evening C-rations, Billy, Phil, Manny, and I were assigned to set up an ambush. I had gotten to know these three men and we got along very well. What we thought would be another routine ambush turned into a situation that could have ended very badly for all of us. We gathered up our weapons, extra ammo for Billy's M-60, and a couple of claymores. After it got dark Phil led the way as we crept out about 200 meters from the platoon NDP to a junction in the trail and set up two well-camouflaged claymores to cover the trail. After we screwed the blasting caps into the claymores, we strung the detonation wire up the hill on the side of the trail and hid in the brush. We kept the clackers for the claymores right next to several grenades that we carefully set next to our position. The clacker was a small electrical generator that, when clicked, produced a spark that ignited the blasting cap and set off the claymore. Blowing claymores and chucking grenades at enemy soldiers in the dark would not give away our position like firing rifles would. They were our last resort if things really hit the fan. Everything went smoothly, but the mosquitoes were especially fierce that night. There was enough moonlight to see fairly well and the lizards and insects gave us their usual serenade. About 0200 hours, Phil was on guard and gently shook Manny and me as we slept. He whispered that he had heard sounds on the trail below us and thought he had seen something move. With our hearts pounding, all of us strained our eyes to see if there was something real on the trail or if he was imagining things. I grabbed the detonator for the claymore that we had set up next to the trail and prepared to blow it as soon as we saw a target. After what seemed like hours, two NVA soldiers crept slowly down the trail, away from the area where the rest of our platoon had set up for the night. Just seconds before I could hit the detonator for the claymore, one of the men whispered, "Wait!" Just then, we saw the rest of the NVA column approaching, probably about 20 men. We let them pass in silence, hoping that they could not hear our hearts pounding, even though we were at least 25 meters from the trail. If I had blown the claymore, it would probably have killed the first two men that we saw, but the others might have discovered our position and returned fire. Three of us against 20 of them would have been very poor odds. They disappeared in silence and we barely breathed for 30 minutes, then sent in a SITREP on the radio. We were told to remain in place until morning and to continue our observation of the trail. There was no further movement on the trail, much to our relief. Nobody slept the rest of the night, and when the morning light finally started to filter through the dense jungle canopy, we silently gathered our gear and prepared to rejoin the platoon.

I began to get acquainted with the men in the platoon and learned where they came from back in the world. The officers in the company tended to be in their mid- to late 20s and were college graduates, as were a few of the draftees like me. About 25 percent of the men in the unit were draftees; most of the rest were 18- and 19-year-old men who had enlisted in order to fight in Vietnam. The men in the platoon, about 20 percent black or Hispanic, came from all over the United States. They were from both big cities and from the country, but the majority came from blue-collar families in small towns and rural areas, mostly in the South. Most of the men seemed to be ambivalent about the war, and political discussions were rare. Surviving for a year and returning home in one piece was the chief concern most of the men had, and many conversations centered on what each man was going to do when he returned home. Almost none of us really understood the intensity of the war protests going on back in the United States. Like me, almost all of the men were in for a real shock when they returned.

Most of the men in the platoon never became close friends and I was no exception, but I did share a closer relationship with the other six men in my squad. Besides the squad leader and myself, there were three young guys from the South and two black guys, one from Florida and one from Massachusetts. Billy, who was from Alabama, was our machine gunner, and his assistant, Manny, was an 18-year-old from the hills of Tennessee.

Billy was short and stocky while Manny was tall and lanky. They were quintessential "good ole boys" and usually kept the squad in stitches with their antics. Phil was an older guy from Missouri who seemed to ride herd on Billy and Manny, and when all three of them got going it was often hilarious. David grew up in Florida and we seemed to hit it off right away, talking about our backgrounds and what it was like to grow up where we lived. Charles was from the ghetto in Philadelphia and was one of the most amiable men I ever met. He often joked that when he got back to Philly he would "run a string of ladies," so everyone nicknamed him "Pimp." All of us bantered back and forth and talked about our plans for the future, but it never got more personal than that. It seemed that there was almost an unwritten rule prohibiting close friendships, because the loss of a close friend was devastating.

Mosquitos were a constant problem, especially at night. If I covered my head with a poncho, it got so hot I couldn't breathe. But if I exposed my skin, the mosquitoes tried to eat me alive. We had insect repellent that was 100 percent DEET and it worked to some degree, but putting it on sweaty skin burned like fire. We also took two different kinds of pills to prevent malaria. One was a small white pill that was taken weekly and was supposed to prevent the deadly falciparum variety of malaria, while the other was a large orange pill taken daily that prevented a more common type of malaria. A lot of soldiers, myself included, did not always take the orange pill because it caused diarrhea.

Everyone hated the land leeches more than anything else. They lived just about everywhere on the moist jungle floor and whenever we stopped to rest, the ugly critters tried to crawl onto our skin and often succeeded. The little buggers were only about an inch long but swelled up considerably after they feasted on blood. Fortunately, one shot of insect repellent caused them to drop off and die. However, they injected an anticoagulant when they attached themselves, so after they were removed, the blood kept flowing. I remember waking up one morning with about a dozen leeches attached to my face and neck. As one of my buddies put it, I looked like a zombie from a horror flick.

Keeping clean was almost impossible since water was often scarce and could not be spared for anything except drinking. We usually wore the same jungle fatigues for an entire mission, and the daily soaking with sweat and the dirt left them filthy. If one was unfortunate enough to have torn the seat out of his pants, that was too bad. I saw more than one grunt walk around for a week with his bare rear end exposed. Because of the heat and the lack of availability, almost nobody wore boxer shorts. The dirt and unsanitary conditions often resulted in skin problems, mainly ringworm and jungle rot. We were treated with liquid Desenex for ringworm, and it worked fairly well but burned fiercely when it was applied. Jungle rot occurred when insect bites or scratches got infected with various jungle bacteria. This resulted in quarter-sized pus-filled sores covered by big scabs that occurred on just about any part of the body. These sores were often treated by having the scabs removed with a scalpel and the wound washed with hydrogen peroxide and bandaged. When the wound finally healed, it left a purple mark that lasted a long time. I had these marks all over my arms and neck, and I got some strange looks when I returned to the United States.

Most of the permanent bunkers built on the firebases were infested with large rats and other vermin. On more than one occasion I woke up with rats scurrying over my legs. During one of our frequent deployments on Firebase Bastogne, I woke up with a large rat sitting on my chest, staring me in the eyes! Fortunately, nobody I knew was ever bitten by a rat, but I heard that some men in other platoons had been bitten. One of the men in the 2nd Platoon was stung by a large scorpion one morning after chow, and he became so sick that he required emergency evacuation to a hospital in Da Nang. The daily grind and the miserable living conditions were in many ways the worst part of my tour of duty. Like one of the guys in the platoon was fond of saying, "It's the little shit that will get you."

The country of Vietnam was rich in wildlife before the war. Species that roamed the mountains and jungles included elephants, muntjac deer, banteng ox, horned wild cattle called gaur, wild boar, leopards, tigers, asiatic bears, various monkeys, and rare apes. There were plenty of snakes including cobras, pythons, and the feared bamboo viper. Bird life was abundant and included ibis, eagles, vultures, hornbills, and numerous smaller birds. Unfortunately, much of the wildlife was decimated by the war or driven into inaccessible places where few men ventured. Huge numbers of bombs were dropped on the Ho Chi Minh Trail and on many remote jungle areas in an attempt to choke off enemy supply routes. During my tour, I saw a few deer, some wild boars and a few monkeys. I never saw a live tiger but did see a set of tiger tracks in the mud along a jungle creek one day when I was walking point. Since I was then and still am a wildlife enthusiast, just seeing those tracks was a thrill for me, and it took my mind off the war, if only for a brief moment. I only saw two snakes during my entire tour — a beautiful emerald-green bamboo viper hanging from a tree along a jungle trail and a large python that must have been at least 10 feet long that we saw hanging from the rafters inside an old temple. The insect life was fascinating and included foot-long centipedes and millipedes, nightcrawlers the size of small snakes, and large spiders. The triple-canopy jungle was beautiful, and I often remarked that it was a shame to be blowing up all those valuable mahogany, teak and banyan trees to clear landing zones for the helicopters. If it were not for the war, the country would have fascinated any naturalist.

Much of the wildlife, including tigers, elephants and rare apes, has returned to the more remote jungle and mountain areas since the war ended. The Vietnamese people have commendably established several parks and preserves to conserve wildlife. Sadly, however, many wildlife species in Southeast Asia, including Vietnam, are threatened by habitat loss and by hunters and poachers who kill the animals because of greed, ignorance, and superstition.

In the steep, mountainous jungles the heat was a big problem, often reaching well over 100 degrees during the day. Every man had to be very disciplined with his water because a water source was not always close at hand. It was great to come to a small jungle stream and have the opportunity to refill our canteens. We usually added an iodine tablet to purify the water and some Kool-Aid to kill the taste of the iodine. Climbing up and down the steep mountains through nearly impenetrable brush and wait-a-minute vines that clung to your body and ripped your sweat-soaked fatigues was a daily event in the bush. My back hurt and my legs felt like lead as I struggled to crawl up steep and sometimes slippery jungle trails. It could get quite cool in the mountains at night, especially during the monsoon season, and more than once I sat huddled in my poncho liner shivering in the dark and trying to stay warm in my wet fatigues.

Food in the field or on the forward firebases, with the exception of a rare hot meal, was mostly C-rations. These rations consisted of a can containing a main meal like spaghetti or beans and franks, a small can of crackers with peanut butter and jelly, a canned fruitcake, fruit, or other dessert, and an accessory pack that contained four cigarettes, matches, gum, toilet paper and instant coffee or hot cocoa. On longer missions we were issued lurp rations, which contained dehydrated meals like beef and rice or spaghetti instead of canned food. They were quite tasty and were very much like the backpacker's freeze-dried meals available today. Most of the men preferred lurps to C-rations, but they required hot water to rehydrate them. Water was often scarce and heating it was not always practical, so we sometimes had to eat our lurps dry. We put empty cans and other garbage into the bottom of our foxholes and buried it just before we moved out. Rumor had it that the NVA would use empty cans to create booby traps, and we did not want to leave them anything they could possibly use.

Even though the forward firebases were not quite like the bush, they were not a great deal better as far as comfort was concerned. They were usually located on hills or mountaintops that were cleared by bulldozers.

Terrain south of Firebase Birmingham.

Bunkers, tents and artillery positions were all surrounded by row after row of trip wire and concertina wire. Each firebase had a helicopter landing pad, an aid station, a communications bunker, and a central headquarters bunker along with mess and supply tents. We got hot chow and showers on occasion, but sleeping in or near the bunkers was only marginally better than sleeping on the ground in the bush. The bunkers were made of logs and corrugated steel and were covered with sandbags. They would stop shrapnel and bullets, but if a rocket or mortar round made a direct hit on a bunker when you were inside, your luck had just run out. The best part of being on a firebase was the fact that there was not only a lot of firepower available, there was a perimeter of razor-sharp concertina wire between you and the NVA. The wire perimeter did offer a certain degree of protection, but it was probably as important mentally as it was physically. It just seemed safer even though there were many examples of firebases being penetrated by sappers or being overrun entirely by larger NVA units. During my tour in Vietnam, Firebases Airborne, Henderson, and Ripcord were all overrun by the NVA and soldiers from the 101st Airborne Division suffered significant casualties. Firebases were tempting targets for NVA mortar crews as well and were often shelled on a regular basis.

5

Night Assault

We had been on Firebase Birmingham for about a week getting some refresher training and taking it easy. Birmingham was the first major firebase west of the ancient imperial city of Hue. It sat on a low hill between the Song Huu Trach River and Highway 547, which wound its way west toward the Ashau Valley. It was a fairly large firebase and it was bustling with activity. The red clay had turned to a fine, powdery dust that billowed into the air as Jeeps and other vehicles made their way to and from the base.

The company received training on patrolling and ambush techniques and managed to get in plenty of target practice. We were also scheduled for training in rappel techniques from a hovering Huey helicopter. Recon and other small units often had to rappel into the jungle, but larger units usually did not due to their size. Our CO thought it would be good training for us to have anyway, and he ordered that every man should participate in the training. Since I was generally afraid of heights, I was not thrilled with the prospect of dangling out of a helicopter on a rope. I had no choice, however, so I decided to buck up and do my best. We started out by learning the basics and by rappelling from a steep rock face on one side of the firebase. It was about 100 feet to the ground, but for some reason it did not bother me too much and I did well during several practice runs. Then it was time to board the Huey, which climbed to about 200 feet and hovered while a man rappelled out of each side of the aircraft. I was a little nervous about it, but it was not as daunting a task as I had imagined it would be. When my turn came, the jumpmaster got me rigged up inside the helicopter, then ordered me to hang onto the rope, put my feet on the skids and lean back. He grabbed me by my shirt, said "You're on your own," and gave me a shove. We were rigged to free fall about 20 feet to clear the aircraft, and it was quite a thrill as I fell backward on the slack rope. I made it to the ground without any problems and after several more runs decided that it wasn't so bad. I really enjoyed the experience, and it helped me to overcome some of my fear of heights. That was good since much of my tour involved flying in helicopters, either as part of an infantry assault force or as a door gunner.

The next day we practiced climbing up a wire ladder with steel rungs that hung from the rear cargo door of a CH-47 Chinook helicopter hovering at about 125 feet. Occasionally troops had to board or exit a Chinook helicopter in this manner, but I never had to use the ladder other than for training. That exercise was definitely worse than the rappel training because a lost grip would result in a fall with disastrous consequences. We had to climb the ladder with fully loaded rucksacks and slung rifles. Carrying heavy gear and being blasted with the tremendous rotor downwash

Ladder training with Chinook.

made this a difficult task. The ladder swung back and forth as I made my way up toward the hovering Chinook. About halfway up my arms and legs were aching and I started to wonder if I would make it to the top. Since there was no backing down, I continued upward, made it to the top and was hoisted inside the Chinook. Thankfully, I never set foot on a ladder again during my tour in Vietnam.

Our platoon got assigned to several bunkers on the northeast perimeter of the firebase. These bunkers were our home while we were guarding the base, and we spent most of the days filling sandbags and reinforcing the tanglefoot wire on the perimeter. Tanglefoot was simply barbed wire that we staked close to the ground. This prevented NVA infiltrators from crawling along the ground and making their way through the wire into the base — at least that was our hope. At night we took turns pulling guard duty, two hours on and two hours off. One night a mad minute was scheduled for 0230 hours, and when everyone commenced firing, somebody who did not know what was happening began yelling, "Gooks in the wire, gooks in the wire!" A new replacement troop from another platoon apparently got scared and confused during the commotion. When another soldier approached his bunker from behind, the cherry evidently mistook the man for an NVA soldier and shot him dead. I never did find out what happened to the cherry, though I am quite sure he was reassigned to another unit. After that, everyone was on edge, and platoon leaders made sure that each man was aware of his fields of fire. Vietnam was a very dangerous place, anyway you sliced it.

Because of the boredom and close quarters we lived in, tempers sometimes got the better of men over seemingly minor incidents. I had been on sandbag detail one day and when I returned to my assigned bunker for chow at noon, I discovered that somebody had gone into my rucksack and taken my last can of peaches. Even though it was not a big deal, I became enraged over the fact that somebody went into my personal belongings, but even more so because they took my peaches, which were one of my favorite desserts. I questioned several soldiers who were in the bunker, and it became apparent which one was the culprit. We exchanged harsh words and it escalated to the point that the other man reached for his M-16 and I followed suit. One of the cooler heads in the bunker prevailed and separated both of us before anything serious or tragic took place. After we both calmed down, we exchanged several cans of C-rations and things got back to normal. The incident now seems ridiculous, but at the time, it was not so funny.

During the last day of our week-long stay on Firebase Birmingham, our company was alerted to prepare for a night mission. We were ordered to leave the base on foot after dark and to cross the Song Huu Trach, the west branch of the Song Bo (Perfume River). After crossing the river, we were to proceed to Nui Khe, about three klicks south of Birmingham. Nui Khe was a large hill that was located between the south and west branches of the Song Bo, about 17 klicks south of Hue. "Nui" means mountain in Vietnamese; the U.S. Army simply referred to it as Hill 618, which was its elevation in meters. The NVA had been using Nui Khe to launch B-40 rockets on Hue and nearby firebases, including Birmingham. Our mission was to find and destroy the rocket sites and any enemy soldiers that we might encounter.

The tropical night began to fall quickly after we ate our C-rations and had a smoke. We sat near the helipad below the firebase, waiting for

View of Nui Khe from Firebase Birmingham.

it to get dark enough for us to leave without being seen. It was hot and sultry and the mosquitoes must have gotten the word that there was fresh meat available. Everyone sat around talking softly and smoking while we waited on the pad for the order to move out. Shortly after dark we got the word to move, so we shouldered our rucksacks and headed single file for the river, making sure that our cigarettes were stowed in our helmets to keep them dry. I was third from last in the rear squad as we made a steep descent to the river. The water looked black in the darkness, and as I entered the chest-deep river the cool water felt good. By the time my squad reached the far side of the river, the red clay that formed the steep 50-foot bank was wet from all the previous foot traffic, and it was like grease. Most of the troops had great difficulty climbing the bank, and I slid back into the river at least three times before I finally got enough of a foothold and the determination to make it to the top. By the time the last three of us made it to the top, we were alone. I strained my eyes in the dark in the hope of seeing the others, but I saw nothing and heard nothing but night sounds. My heart began to pound as I stood there in the dark. I was afraid of walking into an NVA ambush, but even more, I knew that if we blundered into the rear element of our platoon by surprise, someone might mistake us for NVA and open fire. Following a frantic search I found what appeared to be a trail in the dark and walked ahead cautiously, scanning the night for any clues and listening for sounds. After what seemed like hours but was only minutes, I almost stumbled on top of the rear guard. He whispered, "Where the hell were you guys? The lieutenant is pissed!" With that, our second lieutenant from New York City, who had just been temporarily assigned to our platoon while L-T was on R&R, made his way back and proceeded in a whisper to chew me out. I was really angry at having been left behind, and I told him he was an idiot and a poor leader for leaving without making certain all of his men had made it up the river bank. He didn't say anything, and I got the impression that he was having a hard time figuring out what to do next. Later one of the men said, "He couldn't find his ass with two hands and a flashlight." The guy was certainly not cut out to be a platoon leader, and I could tell that he was not comfortable in the bush. About a month later he got relieved of command after getting another platoon lost on a mission. A few months after that I ran into him in Phu Bai, where he was manning a vehicle check

Song Huu Trach, crossed during night mission to Nui Khe.

station, and he seemed perfectly happy with his new job. I wondered to myself about how many men in Vietnam had been killed due to incompetent leadership.

After a pause of about 10 minutes the column proceeded to move once again and slowly headed toward Nui Khe. The night was steamy hot, and everyone was soaked with sweat as the incessant mosquitoes buzzed around our heads. Actually, the river crossing had felt good as the cool waters bathed our sweaty bodies. As we walked slowly and halted on numerous occasions throughout the night, all I could think of was how miserable I was and how long I would have to endure Vietnam before I could get on a Freedom Bird and head back home. At one point the column halted and word was passed back to sack out in place. We got a short hour or so of fitful sleep and then continued the slow march toward Nui Khe. Just before dawn, we reached the base of the mountain and halted to wait for first light. When it began to get light, we silently got on line and began to slowly sweep up the mountain. It was steep and the going was slow. Most of the vegetation was 10-foot tall elephant grass, which had sharp edges and cut

Nui Khe Summit, used to launch rocket attacks on Firebase Birmingham.

my arms as I pushed my way through it. After about an hour, we reached the top of the mountain but did not find anyone there. It was evident, however, that an NVA rocket squad had been there recently. We found empty cans of mackerel and other discarded food remains as well as piles of fairly fresh human excrement. We had probably missed a firefight by less than a day. After posting perimeter guards, we dug some C-rations out of our rucksacks and had breakfast. The ham and eggs and the cup of instant coffee tasted damn good after being on the move all night. We sat around most of the morning cleaning rifles and making sure the rest of our gear got dried out a little. There was an old LZ near the top of the mountain because this was not the first time American troops had climbed Nui Khe looking for rocket squads. About mid-morning a flight of Hueys came in to extract the company and insert us into another area west of Nui Khe. Again, army intelligence believed the area they had pinpointed for our insertion was being used by the NVA rocket and mortar squads that had been shelling Hue and the surrounding firebases.

As the fourth chopper in the lift set down on the small LZ, I hopped on board along with four other men in my squad. I was glad to be leaving because it was very hot and humid in the elephant grass and the cool air felt good as we flew further west. I didn't pay much attention to where we were going; every place seemed the same anyway. After a short flight I could see the lead chopper begin its descent into another LZ that was close to a river. As the chopper neared the LZ, I could see it suddenly flare to the side and began to climb rapidly. At almost the same time the word got passed back that the LZ was hot. The first bird had taken small-arms fire and had been hit near the tail, but apparently none of the troops or the air crew were hit. The mission was temporarily aborted while Cobra gunships were called. We continued to circle the area, watching and waiting. In about five minutes, the gunships appeared and began working the LZ over with ARA (aerial rocket artillery) and miniguns. After several passes the Cobras left and we headed back toward the LZ. As the lead ship made its approach the door gunner and crew chief sprayed the LZ with their M-60s. The chopper descended for a landing, but they did not receive any more fire from the LZ. The rest of us followed in sequence and landed without further trouble. We swept the area around the LZ before we began to move out but did not find anything; the NVA had probably left the area before the Cobras blasted the LZ.

After a short break, Alpha Company moved out with the 3rd platoon in the lead. We were following a well-used trail that was about 30 meters from the river. It was very hot but at least the trail was fairly level and we did not have to climb any steep hills. We moved steadily, trying to reach our objective, which was a small group of hills further west. These hills were believed to be the location of the NVA rocket and mortar teams. About 1500 hours the 3rd Platoon had reached the base of the hills and halted for a break. We moved to join them, planning an on-line movement up the hills. With that, there was a loud "ka-boom," then two more in rapid succession as the NVA dropped three mortar rounds near us. Everybody was scrambling for cover as we tried to figure out just where the mortar rounds had come from. Nobody was hit, but some of the newer guys were a little shaken by the sudden interruption of their smoke break.

We got on line and made a rapid movement up the small string of hills and reached the top without any enemy contact. Shortly after reaching the summit, the 3rd Platoon machine gunner opened up and started to spray the brush on the other side of the hill. Everyone hit the dirt, but after a burst of about 20 or 30 rounds from the M-60, it got quiet. The gunner told his platoon leader that he thought he had seen somebody running through the brush so he sprayed the area. A squad went to check the area out, but they returned fairly quickly and reported that they had not found anything. The squad leader stated, "If it was a gook, he made a clean getaway."

We set up our NDP for the night and planned to keep a 50-percent alert since we knew there were NVA in the area. All of us were happy when the CO decided not to send anyone out to set up an ambush, but the whole thing kind of bothered me. The NVA knew we were there and they knew exactly where we had set up for the night. We had not bothered to move our NDP after dark, as we usually did per our standard operating procedure.

It happened at about 2300 hours. I had just finished my turn on guard and was almost asleep when I heard a whooshing sound, then a loud explosion behind me, near the CP (command post). I heard muffled shouting, then another two explosions in rapid succession, "ka-boom, kaboom." I heard somebody yelling, "I'm hit, I'm hit," then a very loud "whoom" as one of the troops hit the clacker and blew his claymore. Nobody had fired a weapon because we were taught not to fire at night unless there was a clear target. The muzzle flash would give away your location and would invite return fire from the NVA. There was an eerie silence, then I heard L-T whispering loudly, "Anybody hurt?" Nobody in our platoon was hurt, but a trooper in the 3rd Platoon had been slightly wounded in the arm by some shrapnel. Everyone was awake the rest of the night, but no further probes of our position or attacks occurred. There was nothing we could do but wait for it to get light so we could see what happened and assess the damage.

The next morning, L-T and the 2nd squad did a recon of our sector but found nothing. The man in the 3rd Platoon who had been wounded was patched up and appeared to be shaken but otherwise in good shape. Another man in the wounded trooper's fighting position had blown his claymore when he saw a shadowy figure moving in front of their foxhole. They found a dead NVA sapper about 20 meters from their position when they investigated after it became light enough to see. The claymore blast had caught him dead center, and he died instantly as hundreds of steel ball bearings shredded his body. While we ate breakfast, L-T told us what had happened. The first explosion had been an RPG that missed its target and hit about 20 feet up in the trees above the CP. The second and third explosions were satchel charges thrown by a sapper, probably the one who was killed by the claymore. One of the satchel charges had wounded the 3rd Platoon trooper.

Right after breakfast we got new orders on the radio and began to cut a small LZ on top of the hill. Most of the trees were small and we hacked them down with our machetes. We only had to use C4 to blow down about four trees to finish clearing the LZ. Later that morning a flight of Hueys picked us up and we flew back to Firebase Birmingham. Most of our missions were little more than a lot of backbreaking work and trudging through the steamy jungle with very little enemy contact. That was just fine with me. This mission was more exciting than most, but most of us preferred the quiet ones instead.

6

Body Count

Firebase Birmingham looked the same as it always did: dusty, dirty, and bustling with activity. As we exited the Hueys that had flown us in from the boonies, we all noticed two Quad-50s parked near the helipad. These were half-tracks with four .50 caliber machine guns mounted on the turrets. We started talking to the soldiers who were sitting on top of the Quads, and they told us that they were going to fire a demonstration in an hour to show the brass what they could do. After depositing our gear in our assigned bunkers, many of us went back down to the helipad to watch the demonstration. In a few minutes, it began. The Quads began firing at some bare hills about 100 meters beyond the perimeter, and all eight of the .50 caliber machine guns were firing at once. It was an awesome sight and the firepower was tremendous. We all hoped that these guys would hang around for a while just in case the base came under attack. As one of the good ole boys from Alabama said, "Them sumbitches will smoke yo' ass!"

That night a band from Australia played in the mess tent after chow was over. They were pretty good, but in reality just about anything would have sounded good to us after being in the boonies. Everyone got two cans of warm Falstaff beer, and even that tasted good. It seems like Falstaff or Carlings Black Label was the only beer we ever got on the firebases, and that was not very often. Somebody remarked that the army must have gotten a helluva deal from those two companies. After the show was over we wandered back to our bunkers and prepared to spend the night as usual, rotating guard duty on a two-hour basis. When we returned to Birming-

Firebase Birmingham.

ham, our grenadier, who had been in Vietnam for nine months, left on a log bird for Phu Bai. He was being transferred to work in the supply tent for the rest of his tour of duty. I had always been fascinated by the M-79 grenade launcher, or "thumper" as it was called. I talked to L-T, and he told me that I could turn in my M-16 and carry the thumper. We had a mad minute scheduled for 0200 hours, and I was anxious to try out the thumper and drop a few HE rounds out beyond the perimeter. At 0200 everyone opened up and began firing during the mad minute, and I touched off a round from my M-79. As I pulled the trigger it sounded like "bloop" or a hollow "thump" as the gold-colored HE round went speeding toward the edge of the concertina wire around the perimeter. It hit and exploded with a loud "ka-wump." I fired off three more rounds during the mad minute, and even though I had not practiced very much with the M-79, I was placing the rounds pretty much where I wanted them to land. I thought to myself, "I like this weapon."

As far as work was concerned, it didn't matter much whether we were out in the bush or sitting on some god-forsaken firebase. There was very

Author on perimeter of Firebase Birmingham. Note fougasse canister several feet behind.

little time to just sit and relax. Life in the bush was brutal. It was a continual battle with heat exhaustion, dehydration, leeches and mosquitoes, and the pain of carrying an 80-pound rucksack all day long. Life was somewhat better on a firebase, but the work did not stop. There were always endless sandbags to be filled and miles of concertina wire and tanglefoot to be strung. On one occasion during a week-long stay on Firebase Bastogne, the sergeant major who was headquartered there decided that the rocks lining the path to his bunker needed to be painted white! Total bullshit, we all thought.

After a few more boring days on Birmingham spent filling sandbags, we packed our rucksacks and went down the hill to the helipad, where a flight of Hueys picked up the 1st Platoon and inserted us into an area somewhere southwest of Nui Khe. Thankfully, the LZ was not hot and there was no evidence of any nearby enemy activity as we fanned out, forming a perimeter. As soon as the entire platoon was on the ground and the Hueys had left, we began to move slowly down a trail into the dank and dark triple-canopy jungle. I was about 10th in the column, just behind the machine gunner, and sweat poured off my face, steaming up my glasses and soaking my jungle fatigues. We had not been moving very long when suddenly, about 800 meters down the trail from the LZ, there was a loud "boom" followed by the "brrrrrp, brrrrrp, brrrrrp" of several M-16s being fired into the surrounding jungle. The lieutenant was yelling "Cease fire, cease fire, dammit," and I could hear the point man screaming in pain. He had triggered some sort of explosive device, probably a Chi Com (Chinese Communist) claymore, that had been rigged with a trip wire across the trail or had been detonated by an NVA trailwatcher. At least part of the charge had hit the point man in the legs and he was bleeding profusely, but our medic quickly got him bandaged up and hit him with a shot of morphine while a medevac was called. We spread out and formed a perimeter around the wounded man, but the NVA, if there were any around, were long gone. The medevac chopper showed up in about 20 minutes, but the vegetation was too dense for a landing, so the crew chief lowered a jungle penetrator (a small metal seat attached to a cable) down through the jungle canopy. The injured soldier, a tall blond kid I did not know, was rigged onto the jungle penetrator for extraction. He began to calm down as the morphine took effect and he smiled and flashed us the peace sign as he was winched up to the hovering medevac. We heard later that he did not lose his legs but that his wounds were severe enough to get him sent back to the United States. Many soldiers talked about getting a "million dollar wound"—one severe enough to get them out of Vietnam but not so severe that it would affect the rest of their lives. The point man had indeed received his "million dollar wound."

After the medevac departed we continued to move very slowly through the area, looking carefully for trip wires or anything else that looked suspicious. The day before we were inserted onto the LZ, an artillery battery on Firebase Birmingham had pounded the area with 155mm rounds. A LOH (light observation helicopter) pilot had reported enemy movement on the trail system and had called in the strike. The heat was oppressive and the wet jungle floor was crawling with leeches that attached themselves to any exposed skin. I tried to keep my glasses from steaming up with limited success and everytime we stopped for a break, I burned leeches off my legs with a lit cigarette. Around 1300 hours we stopped to eat lunch, and after a brief rest we continued on toward the location that had been selected for our NDP. About mid-afternoon we reached a small clearing and the point man immediately spotted three piles of fresh dirt. After closer examination it was apparent that the dirt piles were actually shallow graves. The discovery was reported to headquarters on the radio, and we received instructions to excavate the graves and look for weapons and bodies. About eight men began to dig while the rest of us formed a defensive perimeter around the excavation site. The graves were very shallow and soon yielded three NVA bodies. The platoon sergeant surmised that the dead soldiers had been killed during the artillery barrage. The massive wounds that the dead soldiers had sustained could only have been caused by large chunks of shrapnel. The dead NVA soldiers were evidently buried in a hurry by their comrades, who had then left the area. The platoon sergeant and several other men checked the bodies and scratched around in the graves, searching for weapons and other gear or information, but they did not find anything. The unearthed NVA were the first dead men that I had examined closely in Vietnam. I was just about overcome with revulsion at the sight of the mangled, waxy-looking corpses with bugs crawling on them. The bodies had begun to bloat in the heat, and the stench of death was nauseating. I will never forget that smell as long as I live. I had a strange hollow feeling in the pit of my stomach, and I thought to myself, "This is nothing like the war movies."

We did not bother to bury the bodies again before we left. Several soldiers had propped up one of the bodies and had placed a cigarette in the dead man's mouth. Another body had been decapitated by a large chunk of shrapnel and was sprawled near the excavated grave. The mangled head had been placed on a stake in front of the grave as a warning to other NVA. That sight was absolutely ghastly, and it is still vividly etched in my memory. At the time, it was difficult to have any pity for the NVA soldiers because they were the enemy and were trying to kill us. They were nothing more than dead "gooks."

We moved cautiously along the trail, expecting to be hit at any moment, but nothing happened. After we had moved about another klick we halted for our evening chow, making some noise so that any NVA within earshot would think we were setting up our NDP for the night. It was difficult for me to eat because the scenario that had played out earlier kept playing over and over in my head. It had been a rude introduction to the realities of war for me, and I tried to forget about it but could not. This was the kind of scenario that no amount of training at Fort Campbell or Fort Polk could have prepared me for. After it got dark, the platoon moved down the trail about 200 meters and began to dig in for the night. L–T wanted the 1st squad to set up an ambush, so we moved about 50 meters further down the trail and quietly slipped up the slope after we had placed three claymores near the trail. We did not dig any foxholes; we just took up positions on the ground and hunkered down to watch the trail. It turned out to be a long night, as I sat against a large tree in the blackness thinking about the horrible sights I had witnessed. The mosquitoes were draining my blood, and I could not keep from thinking about the head on the stake and the terrible smell of the rotting corpses. I imagined that I could still smell them.

The rest of the night went by slowly as we rotated guard duty, but there was no movement on the trail. Mercifully, dawn finally came. At first light, one new man in our fighting position went back into the brush a few meters to relieve himself. He returned quickly with a wild look in his eyes. He said, "Shit, there's a dead gook laying just behind us!" He had discovered another dead, bloated body. No wonder I thought I could smell a corpse! We radioed in our SITREP and reported the body to the platoon leader. He told us to search the body and head back to the platoon. We did a quick search but found nothing other than the man's rucksack, which contained no ammo or anything else. His buddies had evidently taken his weapon and supplies with them, so we left the body where we found it and hurried to rejoin the platoon. I was so sick to my stomach after searching the dead man and smelling death in the air that eating anything for breakfast was out of the question. All I had was a cup of hot chocolate before we shouldered our rucksacks and headed down the same jungle trail again.

The day started like so many others in Vietnam: nothing but the endless pain of toting a heavy rucksack in the oppressive heat with nothing happening. That changed about mid-afternoon when we got word on the radio that an LOH pilot on patrol had spotted a small bunker complex. He said it was about a klick ahead of our direction of movement and appeared to be occupied. The pilot called in an artillery strike, and we halted our movement and waited. It did not take long before we heard the 155mm artillery shells whistling overhead and then four or five loud "ka-booms" in rapid succession. Shortly after the last shell had exploded, we received orders to proceed on and check out the bunker complex that had just been shelled.

The platoon moved ahead at a rapid pace, and after about forty minutes the point man halted and motioned for L-T to move up and join him. They surveyed the situation for a few minutes, then passed word back that they had spotted the bunkers. L-T told us there did not appear to be any movement or activity, but we were extremely nervous, fearing an ambush. The 1st and 2nd squads got on line and we cautiously began to sweep toward the bunkers with our M-16s on full automatic. The 3rd and 4th squads stayed back in reserve in case we got hit. As we got closer we did not see or hear any movement, and the smell of cordite from the artillery explosions hung in the air. In a few minutes we were in the bunker complex, and right away we could see at least five dead NVA sprawled near two well-camouflaged bunkers. If there were other men with them, they had left the area in a hurry.

The NVA soldiers had been cooking rice for their supper when the artillery rounds struck. There was a large pot that had been knocked over by the explosions and the cooked rice was spilled all over the ground. It was still warm. The soldier nearest the rice pot was leaning grotesquely against a small tree with the top half of his head missing and his brains oozing out. He was missing an arm as well. One of the other soldiers had been completely disemboweled by a large chunk of shrapnel, with his guts laying on the ground beside him. The other soldiers were torn up badly as well, but I was so shocked and sickened by the sight in front of me that I could not look closely at them. The scene we had discovered was macabre, and even though these men were the enemy, I felt a certain sadness. It was a horrible sight that remains etched very clearly in my memory.

The platoon sergeant told Manny, Billy and me to check out one of the bunkers and we proceeded very cautiously, looking for booby traps. I am sure setting up booby traps was the farthest thing from the soldiers' minds as they sat preparing their evening meal, not realizing that it was the last one they would ever eat before they died. As we entered the bunker, we discovered a couple of AK-47 assault rifles, about 400 rounds of ammo,

10 mortar shells and several RPGs (rocket-propelled grenades). There were several sacks of rice and some canned mackerel and assorted other supplies. The men who had used the bunker complex were probably one of the mortar and rocket teams that had been shelling the nearby firebases. The inside of the bunker was somewhat cozy and provided a good view of the trail from the firing portholes. I wondered why the NVA had located the bunkers so close to the trail. I guess they had not expected anyone to patrol that area. There was a photo stuck on the wall that personalized the war for me. It depicted a young Vietnamese woman holding a small child, evidently the wife and child of one of the soldiers. I wondered if the woman would ever find out what happened to her husband.

After we gathered all the information and equipment that we found, the platoon sergeant set C4 charges in each bunker and blew them up so they could not be used again. It was getting late in the day, and we moved rapidly down the trail toward a small hill. When we reached the hill we began digging in for the night, and it was dark before we finished getting our perimeter set up. Everyone was tired, but we stayed on 50-percent alert that night because we knew that there were NVA in the area. Nobody ate supper that night because we did not want to risk making noise opening our C-rations and eating. I was so keyed up from the events that had occurred during the day that I was not hungry anyway. Neither was anyone else.

We were often in the field for two weeks before we rotated back to one of the firebases and spent a week there. This mission was short, because after we had eaten breakfast the next morning we got word from HQ on the radio that we were to be extracted and would be going back to Firebase Birmingham. We shouldered our rucksacks and moved to a small LZ about a half-klick away. After we got there we had a smoke and waited to be extracted and flown back to Birmingham along with the cache of weapons and ammo we had recovered at the bunker complex. I was really glad to be getting out of this area and back to civilization, such as it was.

It wasn't long before we heard the choppers coming and marked the LZ with colored smoke. I jumped on the third Huey that landed, along with five others from my squad, and we lifted off toward Birmingham. The flight was only about a half-hour, and I enjoyed the cool breeze that blew through the open doors as I watched the green jungle pass by far

Author near bunker on Firebase Birmingham.

below us. As we approached the landing pad on Birmingham I could see the river we crossed a few days earlier. I thought about the events I had experienced and about the dead NVA soldiers I had seen. My first experience with the enemy weighed heavily on my mind and I had a lot of thoughts floating around in my head. I was really glad that it was them and not any of us that had been killed. We touched down, and I jumped off the Huey and headed up the hill toward the bunkers that would be our home for the next few days.

I was assigned to a bunker on the northwest corner of Firebase Birmingham. It sat just below a large rock outcrop on a point and the location gave us a good view of the steep slope below us. Manny, Phil, Billy, and two new guys that I did not know also shared the bunker. Because our bunker was in a strategic location on the base, it was equipped with a .50 caliber machine gun that was mounted in front of the turret that sat on the bunker. Manny carried the M-60 machine gun in our squad, but he was anxious to try out the big .50 caliber gun. All he could say was, "Damn, I hope there's a mad minute tonight, I wanna fire this baby!"

The bunker was large and well-constructed with good firing ports and a turret on top. Normally we did not sleep inside the bunkers unless the weather was pretty bad because they were prime targets for RPGs and satchel charges. Most of the time we slept behind the bunkers or on top if the weather was nice. After we had eaten C-rations for supper, we sat around smoking and talking. I learned a lot about these guys and even though most of them were regular army and not draftees like Phil and me, they were just as anxious to get out of Vietnam and back home safely as I was. Much to Manny's delight, L-T had made his rounds and told us that there would be a mad minute at 0200 hours. At 0145 we were all waiting for the flare that would be fired to signal the mad minute. At 0200 the flare was fired and the base came alive with small-arms fire. Manny opened up with the .50 caliber machine gun and blasted away into the darkness below the bunker. We even chucked a couple of fragmentation grenades down the hill and heard them go off with a loud "ka-boom!" After the mad minute had ended Manny said, "Wow, that gun really kicks ass! That made my day!"

7

Firebase Bastogne

Firebase Birmingham seemed pretty nice after our recent field experiences and it was good to be back. It was really great to be able to take a shower every day, wear relatively clean fatigues and eat hot chow most of the time. The food on Birmingham and the rest of the firebases was generally pretty good. At least there was plenty of Kool-Aid and iced tea to drink, and anything other than C-rations was a real treat for everyone. Now and then we even got steaks and ice cream. There was usually a movie at night in the mess tent, and I went if I was not on guard duty. The title didn't seem to matter; any diversion from the grind was a welcome change. During our current stay on Birmingham we did get a couple of lukewarm beers the captain had ordered for us and there were even some steaks that we cooked on a makeshift grill. We assumed that our week on Birmingham would be the usual routine of night guard duty and daytime patrols.

Our second night on Birmingham started out like most nights did but at midnight the 3rd Platoon's sector of the perimeter was probed by NVA sappers. They did not make it through the wire because an alert trooper on guard spotted them first. He alerted the rest of the men in the bunker, and they blew the claymores and opened up with the M-60. They managed to kill three of the NVA in the wire but the rest of them escaped. Later that night the NVA dropped a couple of mortar rounds on the base, but they landed near the helipad and nobody was hit.

The next day the 1st Platoon carefully swept the area around the perimeter of the base. The going was slow in the thick brush and it was very hot and humid. Just after we halted for a break at noon and finished

Bunker on Firebase Birmingham.

eating our C-rations, we found an area that the NVA had probably used to mortar the firebase. They were long gone, of course, and we did not find any more sign of them, so we returned to Birmingham at about 1600 hours. The NVA mortar teams usually hit quickly and disappeared before we could get anywhere near them. It was steak night anyway and we were more concerned about getting a chunk of meat than we were about finding some damn NVA mortar team. After we had showers, Manny and I made our way over to the mess tent and each got a big steak, along with some corn bread, instant mashed potatoes, and plenty of green Kool-Aid that tasted great but looked like anti-freeze. It was a great night, no doubt about it.

After three days on Birmingham, we got orders to move to Firebase Bastogne, which was a few kilometers to the west of Birmingham, toward the Ashau Valley. We gathered up our gear about mid-morning and moved down to the helipad area, where we boarded transport trucks for the short ride on Highway 547 to Bastogne. There seemed to be something big in the air, and a rumor was circulating about an impending move back into the Ashau Valley. We all hoped that scuttlebutt was not true.

Firebase Bastogne.

Firebase Bastogne had been named after the town of Bastogne in Belgium. In 1944 the German army had surrounded units of the 101st Airborne Division there and a famous siege had taken place. I hated Firebase Bastogne because it was smaller and much more primitive than Birmingham. It was nothing but loose yellow silt that was about a foot deep, and turned to gooey mud when it rained. The bunkers were not nearly as well constructed as those on Birmingham, and in my opinion, the ground around the base was too gentle to be safe. The jungle was too close to the perimeter and a large force of NVA could have overrun the base fairly easily. I felt very uneasy that only a couple of rows of concertina wire and some tanglefoot were the only defense between us and the dark and foreboding jungle that surrounded much of the base.

Our platoon provided the perimeter guard for the artillery placements on top of the firebase, and we patrolled the area around the base during the day. The jungle was fairly heavy around Bastogne, but it had been sprayed with Agent Orange. That cleared out some of the brush so that we could see a little better, but at that time none of us were aware of

Terrain west of Firebase Bastogne.

the potential hazards of being exposed to Agent Orange. On the days that our platoon was not on patrol we filled sandbags and laid new tanglefoot and concertina wire around the base perimeter, hopefully to prevent sappers from penetrating the base at night. For some reason I never had a good feeling about Bastogne, though I spent a fair amount of time there during my tour.

About the second or third day it was raining fairly hard, the wind was blowing, and all of us on wire detail were soaked and cold. While we were in the perimeter area laying the wire, a tall, wiry man with no shirt came over to help and pitched right in. We did not recognize the man and assumed he was a new cherry who had just joined the company, though he appeared to be older than we were. Phil was very unhappy to be working out in the rain and commented loudly, "I suppose all the damn lifers and brass are up in the mess tent drinking coffee while we bust our ass in the rain." He looked at the tall man and said, "You must be new, huh? What do you think of this shit?" The man replied that it was tough, unpleasant work but that it had to be done. Then he let us know that he was the new battalion commander. Just about everyone's jaw dropped, especially Phil's, but the new commander assured us that he understood our frustration. We could not believe that a lieutenant colonel was out in the rain stringing wire with the rest of the grunts. He told us to be at ease and he visited with us and discussed the situation on Bastogne before he left. After that, we all had a lot of respect for our new battalion commander, who was leading by example and was not afraid to get wet and muddy with the troops. Some months later when he rotated back to the United States and was replaced by a new battalion commander, we all realized just how much we had respected him and his leadership ability.

His replacement was a short, fat man who tried to give us the impression that he was a tough, ass-kicking SOB, but it just didn't work. When he took command, we were ordered to stand in formation as he landed in front of us in his LOH and jumped out, as if to impress us. He almost fell down as he exited the helicopter and then proceeded to tell us how, under his leadership, we were going to "kick ass and kill dinks." Most of the men thought he was a clown and had trouble keeping a straight face. Luckily he didn't remain as battalion commander very long. He rotated to the rear and was stuck behind a desk, where he should have been in the first place.

On several occasions during our many deployments on Bastogne and on other firebases, we were visited by young women who worked for the Red Cross. They were affectionately referred to as the "donut dollies," presumably because they brought donuts and coffee with them for the troops, but most of us never saw donuts or coffee. These young ladies' mission was to cheer up the troops and bring a little bit of home with them. Besides giving us the latest news, there was usually a guitar that someone played and everyone sat around and sang songs. Mostly we just sat around and talked, happy to see some "round-eyed" women and have the chance to flirt with them. The whole thing was a welcome diversion from the boredom. Other entertainers came out to the firebases to sing or tell jokes, but that did not happen very often. Most of the rock bands and other entertainers stayed and performed on the larger rear-area firebases and camps.

During our current deployment on Bastogne, we had the bad luck to get a new company commander, a young captain who really wanted to appear to be tough and gung ho. He ordered everyone on full alert every night with nobody sleeping. That was really not possible, so the squads all worked out a plan. Some men slept while the men on guard not only watched the perimeter, but also kept an eye out for the captain, who swore he would court-martial anyone caught sleeping. He seemed like kind of an arrogant son of a bitch to me, and most of the men took a real dislike to him. My confrontation with him was yet to come.

The new captain joined the 1st Platoon on a patrol near the base one day and almost created a disaster. We had been moving slowly for about an hour when the point element surprised an NVA trailwatcher who had been resting next to a large tree about five feet from the trail. The gook saw our point man too late and never had a chance. As he tried to raise his weapon, both the point and slack men opened up with their M-16s and killed the trailwatcher. They took his AK-47 assault rifle, and while they were admiring it the captain approached them and said, "I'll take that rifle." They turned the rifle over to the captain, and as he moved off with it both of the men had some choice words for him. They knew that we could not keep captured weapons and had to turn them over to battalion HQ, but somehow the idea of him coming up and taking the weapon really pissed them off.

When we stopped around noon to chow down and to take a short break, the captain, without telling us what was going on, went over to the edge of our perimeter and proceeded to fire the AK-47 that we had captured that morning. When he opened up, men were grabbing weapons and diving for cover, not knowing just what kind of hell was breaking loose. An AK-47 has a distinct sound that one never forgets after that weapon has been fired in one's direction. Most of us thought that we were being fired on, but soon the clip was empty and the captain strolled back toward us. With that the platoon sergeant, a crusty old Hispanic guy named Roberto, had seen enough. He sauntered over to the captain and proceeded to chew him out, yelling, "Don't ever pull a stunt like that again, Sir! You're lucky someone didn't blow your ass away! You don't do shit like that!" The captain probably realized his mistake, but other than a mild apology, he didn't say anything. Over time, he seemed to moderate a little as he gained a better sense of the situation we were in and got some experience in how to lead a company in combat.

I really liked our platoon sergeant, Roberto. He was a tough old bird but very fair, and the safety of his men was his highest priority. On one patrol near the base, local kids kept approaching us and tried to sell us Cokes. One of the guys, a redneck from Wyoming, became irritated with a young boy who kept pestering him, and he smacked the kid on the arm with his rifle butt. Most of us liked the kids and that pissed us off. Roberto had witnessed what happened, and he proceeded to really chew the redneck's ass for being a jerk. He ended up by telling him, "If I ever see you pull some shit like that again I'll personally kick your ass and you'll be walking point the rest of your tour. Do you understand me, Dickhead?" That was the only mistreatment of civilians that I witnessed during my tour in Vietnam. Most of the guys liked the kids and other civilians and we did not harass them. The 101st was pretty good about treating the local people decently, and we did not have too many problems with local VC. Our enemy was almost entirely hardcore NVA troops from North Vietnam.

Just about every night while we were on base, one squad was assigned to set up an LP (listening post). I never liked this duty, and neither did anyone else for that matter, because it put the squad in a very vulnerable situation. Three or four men would slip out through the wire after dark and go to a predetermined spot and hide. Their job was to listen and watch for any enemy movement and radio a warning to the base that there were unfriendlies heading for the wire. If the squad was discovered by the NVA, they were pretty much dead meat. At the same time, the squad was also vulnerable to artillery short rounds from the base and errant small-arms fire. It was kind of like being in no man's land.

One night during our stay on Bastogne, Manny, two cherries and I drew the short straw and got assigned to set up an LP. We were supposed to slip through the wire after dark and head for a small grove of trees about 400 meters from the perimeter. I really did not like this setup at all because I was sure that the NVA knew we used that area to hide in since it was the only real cover around. I told L-T about my misgivings, and he was in agreement. We discussed the situation and our options, and after some thought he told me to take the team out only about 100 meters to a small ravine and lay low. Our plan was to send in SITREPS (situation reports) as if we were in the grove of trees where HQ wanted us to set up. Just after dark we carefully slipped through the wire and silently made our way to the ravine. We hunkered down and got set up, preparing for a long night. We began to send in SITREPS on the radio every half-hour as we listened for movement in front of our position. It was too dark to see very much and it began to rain lightly. We could hear the 105mm and 155mm artillery rounds as they were shot and whistled over our heads on their way toward some distant coordinates. About two or three hours after we got set up in the ravine, a 105mm artillery round from the base dropped short, impacting about 30 to 40 meters from the grove of trees in which we were supposedly located. Now we had a problem. If we did not respond, HQ personnel would know that something was fishy, so we waited a few minutes and got on the radio, acting as if we were really agitated.

Manny whispered in the radio, "Cease fire, dammit! That round nearly hit us. Our position is now compromised, request permission to return to the perimeter." After a pause, we received permission to head back to the base, but we waited for 10 or 15 minutes to account for the extra distance to the grove of trees that had been nearly hit by the artillery round. We moved slowly and made it back to the wire, letting the perimeter know on the radio that we were coming back in to base. When we got back to the command bunker, we had to do a great job of acting as if we were really pissed off about having the short round dropped so close to our position. Nobody other than L-T and the four members of the LP knew what had really happened. Manny and I swore the two cherries to secrecy under the threat of bodily harm. I am convinced that if we had set our LP in the grove of trees we would probably have been hit with shrapnel and sustained casualties. After that incident, HQ abandoned the idea of setting up LPs in that grove of trees and in fact it was bulldozed down a few days later.

The next day right after breakfast, L-T took the 1st Platoon out beyond the firebase perimeter for what was to be a short patrol and some planned weapons training. We entered a wooded area and had not gone more than 200 meters when a new guy walking point yelled "gooks" and opened up with his M-16, but in the excitement he missed his target. We briefly saw three NVA soldiers hauling ass down a narrow trail. Several other men fired on them with their M-16s but missed, and the NVA disappeared over a ridge and were gone. We followed the gooks cautiously and looked for them for about an hour, but we never saw them again. Evidently, they had been watching the firebase. It was almost noon and we were about two klicks from the base, so we chowed down and began to head back toward Bastogne. Our progress was slow as we pushed through the heavy jungle vegetation in the sweltering heat. We halted for a rest around 1400 hours, and after a drink from our canteens, we sat around smoking and relaxing. All of a sudden there was a loud "ka-boom" and everyone dove for cover. One of the men was yelling, "I'm hit, I'm hit" as we tried to figure out what was happening. There were no more explosions as we hunkered in the brush, and L-T ordered everyone up. The man who yelled that he was hit was OK and was moving around. He had apparently been hit by some flying debris from what we thought was a satchel charge thrown by a trailwatcher. The man was not seriously injured, so we prepared to head back to Bastogne. The trailwatcher who had thrown the satchel charge had no doubt taken off quickly and we never saw him. We got back to the firebase around 1600 hours and hit the showers. After cleaning up, we headed for the mess tent and ate chow. After that we wandered back to our bunkers and prepared for another night of gazing into the blackness, hoping that we would not be hit by the NVA.

The next day the captain decided that the 1st Platoon would go back to the same area where we had seen the three NVA and try to make contact.

This time, however, we would be taking a scout dog and his handler along with us to help find anyone hiding in the area. We moved out early as we had done the previous day, with the scout dog and handler up front with the point element. We made our way slowly, letting the dog sniff around to catch a scent. Nothing happened all morning and the dog did not detect any fresh scent, so we decided to stop and eat our C-rations around noon. Everyone was sitting around eating, but the dog handler and his dog sat off about five meters from the rest of us. The dog was a large male German Shepherd that appeared to be well-behaved.

While I was eating the dog handler got up and wandered off into the brush to relieve himself, leaving the dog tethered to his rucksack. I decided to go over and give the dog some crackers from my C-rations. The dog seemed friendly enough as I began feeding him crackers, but when the dog handler returned, he saw me and said, "Back away from the dog slowly." That statement and his tone alarmed me, and I did just what he told me to do. After I had gone back to my rucksack, I said, "What was that all about?" He told me that the dog was not friendly and had bitten several people. I found out that most of the scout dogs were pretty much one-man dogs and often did not respond well to strangers. The handler told me, "You're lucky as hell you didn't get your arm torn up." We continued our patrol all afternoon but did not see any NVA or come across anything. At 1600 hours we headed back to Bastogne, and the day turned out to be pretty much a carbon copy of the previous day.

The rest of the week went without incident, and every day turned into the one before it. We spent most of the days filling sandbags, stringing new wire around the perimeter, and making sure our weapons were clean and in working order. At times the boredom got almost unbearable, and if it were not for writing letters to just about everyone I knew, I would have gone crazy. Toward the end of the week we got word from the lieutenant that our next mission would take us into the mountains west of Firebase Bastogne, toward the dreaded Ashau Valley.

8

Sapper Attack

It was a rainy, windy day during the monsoon season, but that didn't matter. The men of Alpha Company reluctantly grabbed their rucksacks and weapons and trekked west along Highway 547. The "yellow brick road," as we called it, was a fairly good dirt road that ran from Firebase Birmingham to the Ashau Valley. The real "yellow brick road" was actually Highway 614 in the southern Ashau Valley, but that did not matter to us. We needed our own. The company split into platoon-size elements and continued west about three klicks to monitor recent enemy activity and to engage them if possible.

It rained steadily all day long as the 1st Platoon moved slowly along the road in the mud, checking for any mines that might have been planted by the NVA. Our point element carefully looked for any signs of recent disturbance to the road surface. Any area that looked suspicious was carefully probed with a bayonet to detect anything metallic. It was miserable going, and there was no way to stay dry. The temperature was cooler now that the monsoon rains had started, and when we stopped for a break, I started to feel chilly. Trying to keep a cigarette lit was difficult, and that annoyed most of us because smoking was one of the few pleasures we had in Vietnam. Other than the rain, the day was like all the other endless boring days that characterized much of my tour of duty in Vietnam. Late in the afternoon we halted, and L-T decided that we would head up an incline to the north of the road and eat our evening chow. After we climbed the short slope, we spread out and dropped our rucksacks. We heated water with heat tabs and made coffee or hot chocolate and opened up

Author taking a break during mission west of Firebase Bastogne.

C-rations. The hot beverages tasted really good and helped us to forget that we were soaking wet and as miserable as drowned rats. Before we ate, the usual barter and exchange of various C-ration meals occurred, but it didn't take long for everyone to start chowing down. I had my favorite, canned turkey, and I traded a pound cake for some fruit cocktail. After we finished eating most of us lit up our last cigarette before it got dark and tried to keep the rain from putting it out.

As soon as darkness began to set in, we prepared to move to another location to set up our NDP. That was our standard operating procedure in case we had been observed by any trail watchers or enemy scouts. We moved about 300 meters west along a small ridge that ran parallel to the road and selected a position that appeared to be fairly defensible. The north side of the ridge was steep and covered with large trees, while the south side was a 20-foot roadcut that separated our position from the road below. As usual, we dug about seven or eight foxholes with four men assigned to each fighting position. These foxholes surrounded the centrally located CP (command post) where the lieutenant, RTO, medic, and sniper set up for the night and monitored the radio. We placed the machine gun along the ridge to the west to watch a trail that ran along the ridge. The men at each fighting position set out claymores about 20 meters in front of their foxholes, using care to make sure the mines were completely camouflaged. We had all heard the rumors about NVA soldiers sneaking up and turning the claymores around to face the men in foxholes, then goading them into touching off the claymores and in essence killing themselves. That never happened to us, nor to any other company or platoon in the 101st that I knew about. I suspected that it was just a rumor, but since it was possible and may have happened somewhere, we were cautious anyway.

The night was almost totally black. No stars were visible through the low clouds, and it continued to drizzle, which kept us from drying out. My turn for guard came and it was quiet, except for the usual night sounds. I was soaked and miserable but in spite of that, I was so tired that I dozed off a couple of times, awaking with a start. I listened intently because it was too dark to see, but I heard only the bugs and lizards. After two hours I was relieved by a new guy named Steve, and I tried to wrap my poncho liner and poncho around me to keep warm and dry. It was a losing battle, but I finally drifted off into an uneasy sleep.

About 0300 hours the man on watch in the foxhole farthest from ours fired four or five rounds with his M-16 and began yelling, "Get up! Everybody get up! Gooks!" Almost immediately I heard somebody else screaming and yelling in Vietnamese. There was panic and confusion in the air as men grabbed in the dark for their weapons and tried to figure out what was going on. I thought we were being hit and low-crawled from where I had wrapped up in my poncho. I found my M-79 in the dark, next to the foxhole where I had put it. I opened it up and removed the HE round that would be of no use at close quarters and inserted a shotgun round instead. Nobody seemed to know whether we were being attacked or not because nothing else happened after the first volley from the M-16, and I could still hear someone moaning and saying something in Vietnamese. I was crawling over toward the CP when L-T whispered loudly, "Nesser, get over here with the M-79."

The man who had fired the shots had also crawled over to the CP and told L-T that an NVA scout had walked almost directly into his fighting position in the dark. By the time the trooper on guard saw the gook it was too late to hit the detonator and blow the claymore, so he opened up with his M-16. He hit the enemy interloper in the gut, and the wounded man had crawled away from the perimeter and laid there in the dark, moaning. The rifle fire had already compromised our position, and L-T didn't want any more firing. He was concerned that the wounded NVA soldier might be yelling instructions to his comrades if they were anywhere close. He briefly considered lobbing a grenade in the direction of the wounded NVA soldier, then asked me if I could put an HE round from my M-79 on the man. That would have been risky since the wounded man was close to the perimeter and we did not know exactly where. Before we could decide what to do, the man quit moaning and we assumed that he had died. L-T put everyone on 100-percent alert and told us to keep our eyes and ears open.

I crawled back to my foxhole, which was nearest to the steep embankment by the road, and listened for movement or sounds with the other men in our fighting position. Shortly after the wounded man stopped moaning, we heard what sounded like footsteps running on the road below. Three of us chucked fragmentation grenades over the embankment toward the sound. We heard the grenades explode in rapid succession, "ka-boom, ka-boom, ka-boom," and Steve thought he heard a yell but was not sure. We remained low, hugging the ground, our eyes and ears straining in the dark to see or hear movement near our position or on the road below us. We all laid there with our hearts pounding, afraid to breathe. There were no further sounds on the road below us, and after about 20 minutes the normal night sounds resumed.

About an hour after we had begun our nervous vigil, we heard several loud explosions followed by small-arms fire from the direction where the 2nd Platoon had set up their NDP. The exchange only lasted for about five minutes, then there was dead silence. Shortly after it quieted down, we heard on the radio that sappers had hit the 2nd Platoon with satchel charges, and we were instructed to link up with them the next morning. We were really relieved that we had not been ordered to link up during the night. A platoon blundering around in the dark where enemy troops were on the prowl was not a great idea. The rest of the night went slowly as we sat there in the dark hoping that we would not be hit like the 2nd Platoon. I wondered what had happened and if those men were all right. L-T rescinded the 100-percent alert order and told us to take turns trying to get a little sleep. After all the commotion, sleep was difficult, but I did manage to get maybe an hour of fitful rest.

At first light we quietly packed up and prepared to sweep the area around our NDP. We found the NVA soldier who had blundered into one of our positions, and he was still alive. He looked like a kid no more than 15 years old, and he was scared and in pain. He had no weapon that we could find, but was carrying rice and some documents in his knapsack. I felt kind of sorry for the kid, but there was little anyone could do about the situation. We were all caught up in the insanity of war, just trying to survive. The platoon sergeant tried to question him, but he apparently spoke little or no English, so the sergeant tried speaking French.

The kid must have understood French, because he started to answer the questions he was being asked. All the platoon sergeant could learn from him was that he was a runner and was going to deliver the rice to a nearby NVA unit. He said he did not know where the NVA were, except that they were somewhere in the direction of the Ashau Valley. Nobody believed that, but if he had any more information, he was not telling us. The RTO got on the radio and called in his report and we were told to stand by while a Huey was dispatched to pick up the prisoner. While we were waiting, our medic patched the kid up the best he could, but his belly wound was severe and he had lost a lot of blood. When the Huey set down on the road, we turned the prisoner over to the crew chief, and the chopper took off immediately and headed back toward Phu Bai. A few days later we heard that the prisoner had not given up any more information than what we had learned and that he had died from his wounds. Helluva life for a 15-year-old-kid, I thought.

After the chopper had departed, we scouted the road below the cutbank and found four or five sets of Ho Chi Minh sandal prints in the wet dirt. Steve discovered a blood trail that left the road and entered the adjacent jungle. After following the heavy blood trail a short distance, we did not find a body, and it was apparent that the wounded man probably died and had been carried off by his comrades. L-T had us move in another 100 meters or so to look for any sign of the NVA, but the rain had washed away the footprints and we soon lost the trail. We moved back to the CP and radioed in our SITREP. Everyone saddled up with their wet rucksacks, and the 1st Platoon began to head towards the 2nd Platoon to offer assistance.

It was a cool morning and the drizzle had stopped, but the jungle vegetation was wet and we were soaked soon after we started down the trail toward the 2nd Platoon's NDP. We moved very slowly because our point man did not want to stumble into an ambush, so it took nearly two hours for us to reach the 2nd Platoon. When we got there, it seemed very quiet and men were moving around, packing rucksacks and eating chow. Several men were sitting near the CP with bloody bandages on various parts of their bodies. Nobody appeared to have been seriously injured except for the medic, who had his left arm in a bandage, and it was obvious that he was in pain. His left hand had been blown off. We found out that a small group of sappers had infiltrated the NDP and had detonated three or four satchel (explosive) charges. During the melee one sapper had been shot and killed and one had been hit full force with a detonated claymore that took his legs off near the knees. He evidently bled to death quickly and was laying there in a heap with the other dead enemy soldier. The other sappers involved in the attack had escaped. We all felt bad about the medic, "Doc" as we called him, because he had planned to become a doctor after he got back to Ohio. He was a courageous guy, and I hoped that he would fulfill his dream after he returned to the States. The only other serious casualty was the platoon leader, who had been hit with a small piece of shrapnel in his eye, and had been bandaged up. We set about helping the 2nd Platoon clear a small LZ, and about an hour later a medevac chopper came in to pick up the platoon leader and the medic. The 2nd Platoon was ordered to stay with us and our combined forces were to continue the mission.

Other than the anticipation of running into more NVA troops, the day was like most of the others — long, wet, and backbreaking. L-T wanted to make it to a large hill about four klicks west, and we moved at a rapid pace. We made our way along a small stream for a couple of hours, and at one point the trail narrowed and followed a small ledge that ran parallel to the stream for about 50 meters. There was about a 10-foot drop from the ledge to the stream, and we made our way along the ledge slowly and carefully. I thought we were sitting ducks as we crossed the 50 meters of ledge, but there was no other good route so we posted guards at both ends of the ledge and proceeded onward. No enemy were around, but one of the men slipped and fell down into the stream, breaking his leg. Luckily it was not a compound fracture, and the man was able to move along slowly with help from his buddies. About an hour after we crossed the dangerous ledge, we came to a small opening in the jungle canopy that looked like it had been used as an LZ before. L-T radioed for a medevac to pick up the man with the broken leg, and while we waited we set out security and ate lunch. Within 20 minutes a medevac landed and picked up the injured soldier, and we moved out again toward our objective. Later that afternoon, we got to the hill where we planned to set up our NDP, but in order to get to the top we had to climb a talus slope for about 100 meters. The going was steep and I slipped about halfway up and banged my shin on a rock. I could hear cursing all the way up as other men slipped and fell on the rain-slicked rocks. After we made it to the top, the hill leveled out and we set up for the night. I felt safe because it was a very defensible hilltop and we had the 2nd Platoon with us, which gave us plenty of extra firepower if we needed it. Luckily, we did not need the firepower and I think everyone got a good night's rest. While we were sitting there having our last cigarette before dark, L-T and I got into a fairly extended conversation. He was no more than a couple years older than I was, and we exchanged our life stories. He had grown up on the west coast, while I was a product of the upper midwest. In spite of that, we had much in common. We had both graduated from college and were married, though he did not have any children. Surprisingly our philosophies were pretty much the same, and it was obvious that both of us would rather have been someplace else. I told him that I had no quarrel with anyone who wanted to be in Vietnam, and that in fact I wished there were more who thought like that. Since I was generally not too much in favor of the war, he asked me why I felt like that. I replied, "If more guys wanted to be here, then maybe I would not have to be here." He replied, "Ness, that's one of the most pragmatic answers I have heard yet."

We spent the next two days moving west but did not make contact with the enemy. They had apparently slipped away after their earlier encounters with us. The monsoon rains had started up again, and we were all soaked and miserable. To make matters worse, all helicopters were grounded due to the weather and could not fly any resupply missions. Just about everyone was getting pretty low on C-rations and cigarettes; our morale was in the dump. We learned later that a storm front had stalled over the South China Sea and had poured more than 50 inches of rain on the Hue and Phu Bai areas, flooding the countryside and grounding all aircraft in I Corp.

On the fifth day of our mission, we got intelligence indicating that a bunker complex had been spotted about a klick to the north of our current position. We were ordered to locate the complex and check it out. L-T decided to have both platoons drop their rucksacks and take only fighting gear while they made their way to the bunker complex. The rucksacks were piled up, and Manny, Steve, David, and I stayed behind to provide security for the rucksacks until both of the platoons returned. At first we were happy we dodged the mission, but after the rest of the combined platoons moved out, it started to get pretty lonely and a little spooky. We talked things over and all of us agreed that if any NVA were in the area they would probably be using the same trail system we were using. If a squad of NVA came across only four of us, we knew that we would be in deep trouble, even though there were two platoons only a short distance from us. We decided to get off the trail and hide in some thick brush, where we could keep an eye on the rucksacks but not be seen if a squad of NVA happened to come along. We waited nervously, but luckily for us, nothing happened. After about two hours we got a radio call informing us that both platoons were returning to our position. The men returned, and as we sat around having a smoke, L-T told us they had found a couple of bunkers, but they were old and had not been used by the NVA recently. After a brief lunch break, we all rucked up again and headed down the trail. Leaving four men alone like that to guard the rucksacks was a really dumb idea in my opinion, but I never said anything to L-T about it. I was just thankful that nothing happened. The next day we made our rendezvous with the rest of the company and continued moving in a westerly direction.

The mission turned into one of the worst I remember. Besides the enemy contact, the rain continued day and night and some large worms came out of the ground after dark and crawled all over us as we tried in vain to sleep. To make life even more miserable, the new captain ordered a 100-percent alert at night so, in theory anyway, nobody was supposed to sleep. After hard physical exertion during the day and little food to eat, that was really not possible. Men at each fighting position worked it out so one man was on alert to watch for both the enemy and the captain while the others tried to get a few winks. Guard duty rotated every two hours. On the third night after we had rejoined the company, things were going as planned at our foxhole. I took my turn at guard, then woke the next man, a cherry who had just joined the platoon. Unfortunately, the man fell asleep during his watch, and the next thing I knew the captain was shaking everyone awake and yelling at us. He demanded to know who was in charge of the position, and I told him that I was the squad leader. He angrily informed me that he was hitting me with an article 15 (non-judicial military punishment), which included a loss of two weeks' pay and a reduction in rank from Specialist 4 to Private First Class. I was pretty upset by the whole thing, but I was responsible for the position and so had to suffer the consequences. As it turned out, I got my rank back within a month, so it was not a big deal, but the article 15 on my service record prevented me from getting a good conduct medal when I left Vietnam. The medal did not mean much to me at the time; all I wanted was to get the hell out of Vietnam.

We had been out in the rain for six days, and our food supply was low to nonexistent. Our original mission plans called for us to be extracted after three days, so we did not carry much extra food. The men all shared whatever food was left, and we cursed the incessant rain as it continued to soak us to the bone. All helicopters were grounded, so extra supplies or getting extracted from the field was out of the question. This had turned out to be one miserable mission! Steve remarked, "All the gooks are holed up where it's dry. Only a bunch of stupid grunts would be out walking around in this weather!" That night the rain poured down and there was actually water running over the ground like a shallow river. We were soaked, cold, and probably close to suffering from hypothermia. I felt as though God himself had abandoned us.

After another three days of endless slogging through the mud and fighting a losing battle with the leeches, we were totally out of food, and everyone was very hungry. The weather had become our enemy now, not the NVA. I dragged on a cigarette, hoping that the smoke would somehow take away the hunger, but it did not. Like many of the men, I had started to feel weak from the lack of food and my spirits were about as low as they have ever been. Our situation began to appear hopeless, and we wondered if the nightmare would ever end. We talked about how we wished there had been a few bunker rats around so we could kill them and roast them up for dinner. One of the men ate some leeches, but they made him sick and he threw them up. Everyone decided that starving to death would not be such a great way to die.

Another day later, the clouds lifted a little and we got word on the radio that a chopper was headed out with hot chow, C-rations and clean fatigues. Everyone was almost giddy with anticipation when we heard the chopper nearing our position and saw it land in a small clearing. It was really good to get dry fatigues and socks, more C-rations and a supply pack with cigarettes, various toiletries and other assorted candy and goodies. We took turns eating hot chow, which was some kind of noodles with tomatoes and hamburger in it, bread, and hot coffee. It was not much, but to us it seemed like a king's feast after starving for three or four days.

UH-1 Huey flying near Firebase Bastogne.

Our spirits soared now that our bellies were full and we had on dry socks and fatigues. Two days later we hastily cleared an LZ and waited for a flight of Hueys to extract us and take us back to Firebase Birmingham. As we popped smoke grenades to mark our position, the sight of the incoming Hueys was very welcome indeed!

We made our way up to the bunkers on Birmingham from the helipad, and the sun actually started to shine after over a week of steady rain. Things really started looking up when we were told there were two cold Falstaff beers waiting for each man along with plenty of cold soda right after we hit the showers. The cooks had been grilling some steaks for us, and we all chowed down on real meat for the first time in months. To top it off there was a movie in the mess tent after it got dark. After a week in the rain, it seemed like we were living high on the hog! Napoleon once said, "An army travels on its stomach." From my experience, that was true.

9

Walking Point

After about five days of the usual boring routine of patrolling during the day and standing guard at night on Birmingham, Alpha Company got new mission orders. A flight of Hueys inserted the company into an AO in the coastal lowlands of the Phu Thu District, southeast of the imperial capitol city of Hue. The Phu Thu District was an area the VC (Viet Cong) used to launch attacks on Hue and Phu Bai. Once we were on the ground, the platoons split and went in different directions, planning to rendezvous in a day or two. It was a new experience for most of us, since all of the missions we had been on since I joined Alpha Company had been in the mountainous areas west of Hue and in the Ashau Valley. We were looking forward to operating on level ground for a change, but we were not very well prepared for the new obstacles that we could encounter. There was a very real possibility that local Viet Cong operatives had set booby traps. Although we were not in the mountains and were relatively near to civilization, this operation turned out to be one of the most miserable experiences I had in Vietnam, and I probably came closer to getting blown away than on any other operation.

It had rained day and night for at least a week, and water was everywhere in the lowlands. As we made our way across the flooded countryside we tried to walk on top of the rice paddy dikes to keep our feet dry, but that was not always possible. Walking on the paddy dikes scared the hell out of me because they were perfect places for Viet Cong booby traps. Our progress was slow the first day as the point element checked carefully for trip wires and anything else that looked like it should not have been there. Late in the afternoon our point man found a small antipersonnel mine planted in the trail along a dike, and we halted while it was rigged with C4 plastic explosive and blown in place. Luckily, that was the only mine we encountered on the mission.

The local villagers in the area went about their daily chores, and it seemed really strange to see Vietnamese people in broad daylight. We had never seen any civilians in the mountainous areas west of Hue, only enemy soldiers. Older men and women worked the rice paddies with docile-looking water buffalo, and they ignored us as we passed by in the steamy heat. The little kids approached our column when we stopped to rest and tried to sell us everything from cold sodas to their older sisters. Some of the teenage girls rode on motor bikes, and the kids called them "cyclo girls." They were obviously prostitutes and tried, without success, to get soldiers to go into the brush with them to conduct business. They almost seemed to be desperate, and in a way I felt sorry for them as they tried to make a living. I suspect that some of the men would have gone with them had it not been for the glaring look of disapproval from L-T. I also wondered how the local villagers got their hands on cold sodas when we never seemed to be able to get sodas at all except for rare occasions when we were back on one of the larger firebases. The black market was obviously alive and well. The little kids seemed friendly and bantered back and forth with us. I was surprised at how well many of them spoke English. Most of us emptied our rucksacks of whatever candy and goodies we had and gave it to them. The older men and women just seemed to glare at us with hollow eyes or ignored us altogether. I wondered whether they appreciated what we were doing or if they resented our presence in their country.

The nights were especially miserable because there were very few good places to set up an NDP and we usually ended up on some small island of land that was not under water. That caused us another problem, because every rat, ant, insect, and snake in the area also ended up on these few dry areas to escape the water, and we had to be on constant lookout for these critters.

As we were digging our foxholes on the second evening of our mission, everyone dove for cover when the men in the foxhole next to ours opened fire with their M-16s. The firing soon ceased, and after the hubbub died down we found out what had happened. A cobra had reared up just in front of the foxhole the men were digging and without any hesitation they immediately blew the snake into oblivion. Before that incident occurred I had not realized that cobras inhabited Vietnam. I wondered how many other cobras were in the area and if we had passed any while we were walking through the rice paddies. Something else to watch out for, I thought. I did not sleep well that night and, like many other men, I thought more about snakes than our real enemy, the Viet Cong.

The mosquitoes were out in force both day and night and were much worse in the wet rice paddies than in the mountains, in spite of heavy applications of insect repellent. When I was not on guard during the night, I tried to cover my face and head with my poncho. That was sort of like getting slowly roasted in a plastic sack, and I found it hard to breathe the hot, musty air. If I uncovered, the mosquitoes were almost unbearable and nearly drove me insane, so I alternated by covering for a while, then uncovering for as long as I could stand it. One night I awoke abruptly when I started to get stung all over my body by something. I soon discovered that I had been sleeping on a low anthill and was under attack by little red fire ants. Luckily, I woke up before they had completely covered me and I was able to quietly rub them off before any real damage was done. The bites were painful and began to itch, but all I could do was put up with the discomfort and find another dry spot where I could sleep. As I laid there in misery I kept thinking about how much I wanted to be somewhere else. The next morning when I told Manny what had happened, all he said was, "Hey, it's just another day in this shithole!"

Every night one of the squads set up an ambush not too far from our NDP. When my squad drew the short straw just after supper on the fourth night, we made plans to go about 200 meters down a paddy dike and into a small hedgerow to set up the ambush. After dark we quietly made our way down the dike to our predetermined position and carefully set up two claymores to form a nice kill zone on the dike. Then we crawled into the hedgerow to wait. We planned to have three men sleep while the other three kept watch and remained ready to blow the claymores if we got company on the dike. It was hot and steamy and it didn't take the mosquitoes and leeches very long to find us. We had heard on the radio earlier that day that the NASA mission had landed on the moon. When my turn at guard came I sat there watching the full moon as it peeked out from behind the low clouds from time to time, and I wondered about a world that seemed to have gone mad. We had the technology and could muster the will to land men on the moon but could not seem to figure out how to get along with other nations and avoid sending young men to be killed and maimed in a seemingly endless war.

About 0300 hours while I was awake and listening to the night sounds, I heard a faint rustle in the underbrush as it started to rain lightly again. I was not sure if I was hearing the raindrops splatter on the vegetation or if it was the distant thunder that was moving closer. Then I heard something again, and it was louder and definitely not the rain or thunder. I poked Steve, who was next to me, and whispered that I thought I heard some movement to our front. He listened intently for a minute and whispered that he had heard something too. We quietly woke up the other four men and informed them that something was moving toward our position. Everyone laid there in silence in a small circle, with each man facing outward. We continued to hear what was definitely something or somebody moving our way, and we got ready to blow the claymores as soon as we could see a definite target. My mind quickly started to go over all the possible scenarios. I convinced myself that some local VC soldiers had probably seen us setting up our ambush and were sneaking up, preparing to overrun our position. My mouth turned to cotton and I could feel my heart pounding in my chest. I just hoped that nobody else could hear it beating.

The sound was quite close now, and it seemed that some major shit was about to hit the fan. All of a sudden Steve poked me and said almost out loud, "Look!" At that moment we all heard a grunt, followed by more grunts, and in the faint moonlight we began to make out the shape of a wild hog moving slowly down the dike toward us. We relaxed a little when we saw the shapes of three or four more hogs moving past us in the dark. Steve whispered in a loud voice, "I'll be damned! Those stupid pigs just scared the crap out of me!" Thankfully, the night ended without further incident, and at first light we checked in on the radio and made our way back to the rest of the platoon. The incident seemed pretty humorous when we got back and told the rest of the guys about it. We took a lot of ribbing, but while it was happening things were very intense, and all of us did indeed have the crap scared out of us. We were convinced at the time that we were about to be overrun and maybe killed. Luckily for us, ambushes seldom yielded results, but the long wait in the dark was nerve-wracking and the "pucker factor" was high.

While we were chowing down on cold C-rations that morning, we received orders to move about three klicks to our north and rendezvous with the rest of the company, which had split off from us when the mission began. Our new mission would be a company-size night movement to cordon off a village that was suspected of harboring both VC and some NVA soldiers. The day was long and hot as we moved slowly through leech-infested water, along paddy dikes and past local villagers doing their daily chores. Most of the people we saw were old men or women and small kids. The kids yelled and waved as they usually did, and the older men and women gave us the sullen, hollow-eyed glare that seemed to be their way of saying they wished we were not there. We never saw young men over about 15 years of age because they were either in the ARVN (Army of the Republic of Vietnam) or were Viet Cong.

We linked up with the rest of the company late that afternoon and took off our rucksacks, looking forward to a smoke and some much needed rest. Everyone sat around in a little grove of trees preparing the evening meal of heated C-rations and coffee and enjoying small talk. The conversation, as usual, was about what we wanted to do when we got back to the "world." I was enjoying some pound cake while Steve was repeating and embellishing the previous night's encounter with the wild hogs when L-T meandered over and gave me the bad news for the day. "Nesser, you're walking point tonight" he said. I had walked point several times before, but never as part of the lead element for a company-sized operation. In addition to that, the fact that it was a night movement had me really concerned. We almost never moved at night for a variety of reasons, but we needed to do so now in order to cordon off the village under the cover of darkness and be ready to surprise and kill or capture enemy soldiers early the next morning.

Walking point was either the most exhilarating or the scariest job in Vietnam, often both. It required every bit of concentration one could muster. When I walked point I usually moved slowly, scanning the jungle ahead of me, looking for anything that looked unnatural or out of place. At the same time, I would carefully examine the trail, looking for trip wires, fresh dirt, or anything that looked suspicious. The birds and insects were often a clue; if they went silent, something was wrong.

I sat for a while with butterflies in my stomach as my thoughts drifted.... *I could see the thick jungle that almost hid the narrow trail I followed as I searched ahead intently looking for trip wires, disturbed soil or anything that looked out of place. I heard the jungle sounds and smelled the dank vegetation. My feelings flip-flopped. First, the hunter's high, then the fear of being hunted....* I quit daydreaming and came back to reality when L-T came over and sat down beside me to discuss plans for the night movement. After we discussed the mission and had a smoke, it was almost time to move out.

We began our slow trek at dusk, just before it became completely dark. I was walking point followed by my slack man, James, then L-T and the 1st Platoon. The rest of the company fell in behind the 1st Platoon. I felt good that James was walking slack, since he was one of the more experienced men in the platoon at that time. He was a huge black guy from somewhere in the South, Georgia I think, and one of the nicest men I knew. If anything went wrong, I knew that I could count on James to back me up or do whatever needed to be done.

I was extremely nervous, and a feeling of inevitability came over me as I started down a paddy dike in the direction of the village, which was about three klicks from our present position. It was getting pitch dark and low clouds obscured the moon. It looked like it would rain some more. Visibility was very limited as I crept slowly along and felt my way along the dike, fearing that I could hit a booby trap at any time. I could not see well enough to discover trip wires or anything else, and I realized that I was little more than a human mine sweeper. There was little I could do other than pray that I did not hit a mine and blow myself and half the squad away.

It began to rain lightly again, and just to add to the misery the mosquitoes greeted us in thick swarms. We made our way slowly, with L-T calling frequent halts to check our bearings and make sure we were on the right dike. A few hours into the move, as we crossed a small expanse of water between two dikes, I stepped into a hole and went into the water over my head. I would likely have drowned if it had not been for James grabbing the top of my rucksack and pulling me out of the hole. We posted a man to warn others of the hole as we continued to move through the darkness and rain. For me it seemed like the nightmare would never end as I kept moving slowly, hoping that I did not step into any more holes or trip a booby trap.

About 0300 hours it began to rain harder and lightning began to flash all around us as we approached a row of trees and brush that paralleled the dike, about 30 meters to our right. The scene seemed almost surreal, and when we were just about opposite the tree line I heard a click, like the bolt of a rifle closing, and I froze in place. At almost the same instant, a bolt of lightning flashed and I heard somebody in the hedgerow yell, "Don't shoot! They're ours!"

L-T yelled, "Dammit! Hold your fire! This is Alpha Company." Everyone held up and stopped as he went over to the treeline to talk to the GIs who were there and get things squared away. After about five minutes he returned with a disgusted look on his face and told us that another line company was operating in the area and that one of their platoons had set up the ambush in the hedgerow, unaware that we would be moving through the area during the night.

I was really shook up and kept saying to James, "Son of a bitch. We walked into an ambush!" I could not get over the fact that our HQ personnel back in the rear apparently had not coordinated the move well enough to keep us from walking into a deadly ambush set by our own troops. Like the saying went, "Friendly fire isn't very friendly!" I have no doubt that if the lightning flash had not occurred just when it did, giving the other troops a chance to identify us, I would have disappeared in a red mist when they blew their claymores to trip the ambush.

L-T was really agitated and very angry that we had been so close to being caught in the kill zone of an ambush, and after a heated discussion with the captain, they both decided that another platoon would take over and walk point for the rest of the rapidly disappearing night. I was pretty shook up and in a daze, and I really can't remember much else about the rest of the move that night except that I was very happy to relinquish the point to someone else. I kept playing the incident over and over in my mind as we slogged on through the mud and water, thanking God that somehow we had escaped the ambush. Even though I knew that walking into the ambush was not my fault, I still felt bad about it and realized that the difference between life and death was a very thin line.

We finally reached the village just before dawn and surrounded it. At first light we swept through the village and rounded up any men that we could find. We detained about four or five younger men and a few older ones. Several ARVN soldiers who had joined us on the mission interrogated the detainees. We watched as they yelled and intimidated the prisoners, striking several of them in the gut with the butts of their rifles or slapping them across the face. The ARVN seemed to be brutal with their own fellow countrymen, and it was easy to see why the local villagers did not like them. In spite of the threats, they discovered nothing. No VC, no NVA and no weapons. If enemy soldiers had been there, they got tipped off and left before we got there. We were all soaking wet, hungry and bone-tired, and really happy to hear that we would be staying in the village for a day or two to rest and monitor enemy activity.

Each platoon was assigned a sector of the village to watch for infiltrators, and my squad got put into an old abandoned Buddhist temple near the edge of the village. We dried off, concocted some lunch from our C-rations, and made hot coffee. After we finished eating we spread our poncho liners on the cement floor of the temple and slept for most of the day. Later in the afternoon when we had finished sleeping, several of us went outside the temple and decided to patrol around the area to see what was there. There were mostly peasant huts and people walking around going about their business. Most of them did not acknowledge us, but the kids came around to talk and get whatever we would give them. We headed back to the temple with plans to cook up a C-ration feast for supper. As soon as we entered the temple we spotted a large python, which appeared to be at least 10 feet long, in the rafters above us. The huge snake did not hang around very long after it saw us — it slithered into a hole in the tile roof and disappeared from sight. We were all a little nervous that night about the big snake in the roof, but we never saw it again. The snake was probably more scared of us than we were of it and very likely made its escape into the nearby jungle after dark.

The following morning we saw that an old lady occupied the hut across from the temple, and it appeared that she lived alone. She was frail but worked all day in her garden and swept the area around her hut with a crude broom. We felt kind of sorry for her, so we gathered up a bunch of C-rations and took them over to her. She was grateful for the food and smiled and bowed toward us, then went into the hut. Soon she returned with some tin cans she used as cups and a pot of warm green tea. She graciously poured each of us a cup of tea and again smiled and bowed as she handed the tea to us. It was not all that good, but not wanting to offend the old lady, we drank the tea and thanked her, bowing and smiling. Later someone joked that the warm liquid might not have been tea at all, but warm pee instead and that we were lucky she had not poisoned all of us. In reality, she was probably like so many other Vietnamese people we encountered who were not political and just wanted to be left in peace to pursue their agrarian lifestyle.

That same afternoon, just as everyone had sacked out in the temple to escape the heat and take a brief siesta, we heard what sounded like AK-47 fire on the opposite side of the village, then heard the "ratta-tat-tat" of an M-60 machine gun firing back. We all wanted to run over to see what had happened, but knew that we could not leave our position. Almost immediately, the radio crackled and we were informed to be on alert for enemy infiltrators. Everyone grabbed his weapon and began watching the edge of the village from our vantage point in the old temple. We did not see any movement at all, and even the villagers had disappeared into their hootches. About a half-hour later, L-T came into the temple and told us what had happened. One of the guys in the 3rd Platoon had spotted a younger man looking under some mats near a hut at the edge of the village. His activities appeared to be suspicious, so the soldier had yelled "Dung Lai!" ("stop" or "halt" in Vietnamese). With that, the young man grabbed an AK-47 rifle from under the mat and fired a few quick shots at the soldier but missed. Then he took off running for a nearby hedgerow, but another soldier who was manning the M-60 drew a bead on the escaping man and cut him down with a short burst. It turned out that the young man killed by the machine gunner was one of the men interrogated the day we arrived in the village. No doubt he had been a Viet Cong soldier. If there were other VC in the village, they maintained a low profile and did not make themselves known.

The next afternoon we saddled up again and hiked out to the main highway about two klicks to the west, where trucks came and picked us up. We were transported to LZ Sally, where we were scheduled to stand down and rest for a week and take some refresher training. That was great news for everyone, and we all looked forward to the rest, showers, and hot chow. I think just about everyone was glad to leave that miserable and dangerous flooded lowland area along the coast. After that mission, the mountains and thick jungle didn't seem quite so bad.

10

Camp Sally

It was great to be back at Camp Sally where we could take showers, eat real food, drink beer at the EM club, and watch movies at night. We were back for some rest and refresher training and were scheduled to be on stand-down for a week. The movies at night were old and not of the best quality, but they were a welcome change from the routine. We still had to take our turn at bunker guard duty at night, but at a relatively large base like Camp Sally, the rotation left us with more nights in our tents than in the bunkers. We all got a chance to go to the PX (Post Exchange) to buy shaving supplies, writing paper, reading material, candy, and cigarettes. There was an Exchange catalog available, with lots of electronics, china, and other merchandise that we could order and have shipped home at very reasonable prices. I ordered two cameras, two sets of china, and some other household items and gifts to be shipped home to Linda.

The training was no big deal, and it helped to pass the time. We took target practice on the range at the edge of camp and reviewed the use of various weapons. We also reviewed and practiced squad maneuvers and patrol tactics, ambush techniques, hand-to-hand combat, radio protocol and first aid training. A .50 caliber machine gun was set up on the target range one day, and we took turns shooting at barrels and a wrecked APC (armored personnel carrier). I was a surprisingly good shot with the .50 cal and had no trouble blasting hell out of an old barrel. The company commander joked that maybe he would have me carry a .50-cal on the next patrol. No thanks, Captain!

Our ARVN interpreter, Tran Thuy, was a great guy and I liked him immediately the very first time we met. During the stand-down he conducted an elementary Vietnamese language course, and everyone had to attend at least one day of language training. I really enjoyed the lessons and found them fascinating. Thuy had a way of making everything a joke, and at times he had us all rolling with laughter. I never learned to speak fluent Vietnamese but could carry on a very rudimentary conversation and understand at least some of what the Vietnamese were saying. Most of them could speak some English, so communication never seemed to be too difficult. Thuy did not understand all of our customs and was quite gullible, so we took advantage of that fact to put him up to various pranks, such as requesting left-handed canteens from the supply sergeant. The battalion commander came to watch us on the firing range one afternoon, and somebody convinced Thuy to go to the commander, salute, and say, "Hey, dude, what's happening?" The commander was not a jovial man and did not appreciate the humor like we did!

Kit Carson Scouts were former NVA or Viet Cong soldiers who had taken advantage of the "Chieu Hoi" (literally, "Open Arms") program and had surrendered to the Army of the Republic of Vietnam (ARVN). Our platoon scout was an interesting character who had been forced into the North Vietnamese army after they had executed his wife. He was sent south along the Ho Chi Minh Trail to fight and switched loyalties the first chance he got. After his "re-education" by the ARVN, he was attached to our platoon. He hated the NVA with a passion and kept us out of more than a few ambushes with some very good advice. The whole theory behind using Kit Carson Scouts was that they were familiar with the territory and knew the habits of the NVA. Some units had their scouts walking point, but Alpha Company never allowed that to happen simply because of the fear they could be double agents and lead us into an ambush. I don't think that fear was justified, certainly not with our scout, but that was our standard operating procedure.

One of the Kit Carson Scouts from another company had been a sapper. Sappers were elite troops roughly equivalent to our Rangers or Special Forces and were especially good at getting through the wire surrounding firebases. During the stand-down the scout gave all of us a demonstration of how he could penetrate a defensive perimeter around a firebase. The area he chose for his demonstration was well fortified with concertina wire and tanglefoot, and none of us thought that any human could possibly get through the wire. The scout proceeded to strip to his shorts, carrying only a fake satchel charge and some small wires that he held in his mouth. He snaked his way along on his back, using the small bent wires to clip strands of tanglefoot and concertina wire together while he twisted his wiry body and made his way through the wire. Everyone was amazed at how rapidly he came through the wire, making no sound at all. In no time, he was inside the compound with his fake satchel charge and would have been ready to wreak havoc had it not been a demonstration. After that demonstration we had a new respect for the enemy we were fighting, and everyone was extremely alert at night while on guard duty. It became very clear that the night was not as safe as we had thought.

That night a rock band from Australia put on a great USO show for us on a makeshift stage. The group was surprisingly good, singing most of the current favorite tunes that we all liked. Besides the band, there were two go-go girls wearing tight nylon body suits, and of course this went over big with all the guys. We had been allowed to bring beer from the EM club for the show, and it flowed freely. Most of the guys were feeling no pain as the group played song after song and the girls danced on stage. Toward the end of the show, a young blond stripper appeared, and her act came close to causing a riot. Everyone at the show seemed to enjoy the brief respite from the war, and after the obligatory singing of the Animals' hit song, "We Gotta Get Out of This Place," the show ended. Men gradually drifted back to their tents and crashed on their cots, tired and full of beer.

Several loud explosions rocked me out of a sound sleep at about 0200 hours. After the first of several explosions, I heard cries of "Incoming! Incoming!" and then more loud "boom-boom-boom" sounds. Besides me, several other men had been startled by the blasts and we began to knock sleeping men off their cots and onto the ground. I hugged the ground trying to make myself small as several more mortar rounds exploded very close to the tent. I could hear shrapnel whine by overhead, and I heard several chunks rip through the canvas tent. As suddenly as it began it was over, and men were milling around trying to find out what had happened. We found out that our sector of Camp Sally had been hit by mortars and RPGs. The shrapnel had ripped a number of holes in our tent, and it looked a little like swiss cheese toward the top. Luckily, nobody in our tent had been hit. Some rear-echelon soldiers who were permanently assigned to the base had taken shelter in a bunker about 20 meters from our tent. Unfortunately for them, a mortar round hit right in front of the opening to their bunker. I watched as the medics were extracting them from the bunker, and it was a mess. They were very badly hurt, and there was blood everywhere. A couple of the men were moaning and crying, but it was obvious that some of them were no longer alive. We found out the next day that three men were killed and two had been severely wounded and were being shipped to Japan. It seemed that whether you lived or died was often a matter of inches and a lot of luck.

The next morning the 1st and 2nd Platoons from Alpha Company were ordered to sweep the area west of Camp Sally and look for the NVA who had hit the base during the night. The area was mostly low, rolling hills that were covered with brush and small trees. There was one higher hill that we suspected was the source of the mortar fire, though the RPGs

Mission along Rao Nai River.

had no doubt been fired from much closer range. We left our rucksacks behind and carried only weapons and extra ammunition along with our canteens. There was not a cloud in the sky as we began our sweep in the scorching heat, looking for any evidence of NVA in the area. After several hours we were soaking wet and L-T called a halt so we could rest and relax for a few minutes. Everyone took a few swallows from his canteen and lit up a cigarette while we tried to take advantage of some shade from a few larger trees. Steve had just walked off into the brush to relieve himself when he came running back toward L-T. He was excited and said, "I saw some gooks heading up that big hill just ahead. I think there were about four of them." We peered at the hill, which was about 150 meters from our position, but did not see any movement. Steve said again, "I swear I saw them." L-T got on the radio and called for an air strike. Within about 20 minutes we heard two F-4 Phantom jets heading toward the big hill. L-T was in contact with the pilots and advised them of our position so they did not roll in on us by mistake. With that, they zeroed in on the hill and dropped napalm. The hill lit up like the Fourth of July, and even at 150 meters we could feel the heat from the strike. After two passes, the jets left to return to their base and we worked our way toward the hill. It was still burning and we did not want to risk getting anyone in the platoon hurt, so we held up and observed the hill for about a half-hour.

There was no movement of any kind, and if there had been any NVA on the hill, they had been turned into crispy critters. L-T reported no further movement or signs of NVA, so we were told to head back to Camp Sally. The cold showers felt really good when we got back.

That evening everyone was tired after the long day and nobody seemed too interested in going to the EM club. After evening chow, several of us went over to a hootch next to the supply building to visit an old friend. Jimmie had been with Alpha Company for a long time, but when he got short he somehow secured what we all considered to be a plush job in the rear at Camp Sally. He did nothing but keep the supplies in order and load log birds headed for the bush with C-rations and ammo. Most of us would have done just about anything to trade jobs with Jimmie, but for most of us it would never happen. After visiting with Jimmie about life in the rear, he cranked up his new Akai tape deck and started playing the Beatles song, "Come Together." As the music played, Jimmie grabbed a tambourine from on top of one of the huge speakers and started to dance around, keeping time with the music. Pretty soon we all joined in, celebrating our friendship and trying to forget where we were at the moment. Later that evening, we all headed back to our hootches, and as I laid in my bunk I could still feel the bass from Jimmie's speakers and hear the Beatles singing. What a night, I thought. Here we were having fun when just last night we got mortared and had casualties. I tried to sort it all out in my head, but it did not make much sense. I downed another beer and tried to forget the whole thing.

The rest of the week passed without further incident, and we headed back out to the boonies for what seemed like endless weeks of patrols, night ambushes, sweltering heat, leeches, mosquitoes, and very little evidence of the enemy. Many of the men who had been with the platoon before I joined them in May were gone now. Several had rotated back to the States, and a few short-timers were sent back to Camp Sally or Phu Bai to finish out their tours before heading back to the world. Our squad leader, Rich, went home, and Charles was back at Camp Sally working in the supply tent. Phil and some others had also made it home safely. L-T went back to California, and we got a new platoon leader named Roger. He was a nice guy but kind of aloof, and I never developed a close a relationship with him like I had with L-T. Our new platoon sergeant was a young guy out of Fort Benning, and he did a great job with the men. He was pretty green, but he was willing to listen to some of the old-timers and take advice. He learned pretty quickly, and I respected him and trusted his leadership. I was fairly close with two men who joined the platoon shortly after I did. Greg was a big dude from California, and Larry was a rather quiet fellow from somewhere in Arkansas. We hung around together and made sure that we were in the same squad. Larry was an especially good point man, and everybody felt relatively safe when he was on point. We knew he was not going to flake out and lead us into an ambush or get us in trouble. Larry eventually volunteered to walk point on a permanent basis and did so much of the time, though some of us relieved him now and then.

Another soldier named Steve, who was also from California, had joined us about a month or so earlier, and he became my best friend. He was about my size, had gone to college, and we hit it off right away. Both of us were Bob Dylan fans, and we spent hours discussing the meaning of various Dylan songs. I thought that Steve was kind of a cross between a surfer and a hippie, and he was well-liked by most of the other men, except for our new platoon leader. Steve got into a heated argument with the platoon leader one day over point rotation. As a result, Roger sent Steve out on a one-man LP (listening post) that night. Steve was livid with anger but went out about 100 meters and hid in some dense brush for the night. When he returned the next morning, all he could say to me was, "That son of a bitch tried to kill me and he will pay for it." I was concerned for a while that Steve might try something drastic and get himself into a heap of trouble. It turned out to be an idle threat made in the heat of the moment, and Steve gradually got over it, though he never liked Roger.

I did not know most of the newer troops very well, and I felt uneasy around one guy from the Los Angeles area. He was a skinny, pale-looking guy who had a lot of trouble carrying his rucksack even though his squad leader had not required him to carry any M-60 ammo. To boot, he was some kind of religious nut who was constantly quoting the Bible. He always had a strange look in his eyes, half wild and half fearful, and most of us gave him a wide berth. One day about two weeks after he joined us in the bush, we were cutting our way through some very thick jungle with machetes. He became entangled with vines and started screaming, "Vines, vines, the whole fuckin' world is nothing but vines!" A crazy man screaming in the jungle was not what the platoon needed. His antics put all of us at risk. The medic got him calmed down, and the next day the new lieutenant put him on a resupply chopper and sent him back to the rear to be reassigned. Most of us thought that the guy was either crazy or very clever.

The long weeks seemed like a movie being played over and over, and the routine was monotonous. We had not seen hide nor hair of the NVA for a while and it was obvious that they were avoiding contact with us. The captain seemed to think that they were up to something big and were reserving their strength. Now and then something happened to break the monotony. I was walking point one morning, following a beautiful jungle river. As I rounded a bend and cautiously moved along a small sandbar, I saw a set of large cat tracks that could only mean one thing — tiger! I stopped and strained my eyes, hoping to catch a glimpse of the big cat, but I saw nothing but jungle and the meandering river. If the tiger had been nearby, he no doubt heard us coming and had probably slipped away quietly. We moved along the river all day, and later that afternoon, after posting guards both upstream and downstream, we took turns swimming and bathing in the river. The cool water felt like heaven after the steamy heat had soaked our fatigues with sweat. After everyone had cooled off, we filled our canteens upstream from where we had been swimming and moved out, heading for a small hill where we planned to set up our NDP.

Most of the time patrolling the jungle was just plain hard, boring work — day after endless day. Contact with the enemy was very sporadic, and it was the day-to-day miseries in the bush that got to us. The NVA continued to be elusive and on the run, but the man who was walking point still had to be on constant alert. There was no way of telling if or when he would walk into an ambush or be fired on by a scout or trail-watcher. Luckily nothing happened and the most serious ailments seemed to be ringworm, jungle rot, and dysentery. Like most of the men, my arms and legs were covered with purple welts and scabs from the jungle rot. In

Extraction following mission along Rao Nai River.

some ways I was beginning to enjoy the thrill of the hunt, and after months in the bush I was in very good shape. The arduous treks through the jungle did not bother me as they did at first. Every now and then, however, it would dawn on me that this was no game. There were little brown men all around us whose objective was to kill us if they got the chance. I worried about making it home in one piece when I had time to think, but most of the time I was too busy or too tired.

11

The DMZ

Some months later, November 13, 1969, to be exact, Alpha Company was on its second day of another stand-down at Camp Sally for training, weapons maintenance and rest. We all were issued new fatigues, got haircuts, and picked up supplies at the PX. The weather was dry and sunny so we spent a lot of time firing our weapons on the target range at the edge of camp. While most of the company took target practice, a few of us occupied the observation posts just beyond the range to make certain that Viet Cong snipers did not shoot at the troops. I had a nice knoll to sit on while I watched a small valley below me and caught up on my letter-writing. About 1000 hours, the company clerk came speeding out in a Jeep. He yelled at me to hop in and said that everyone had to get their rucksacks packed and be ready to move out soon. I hurried to our tent and, along with the rest of the platoon, began to make sure my ruck contained the necessary ammo, grenades, claymores, flares and other gear along with a case of C-rations and six canteens of water.

Within an hour everyone was saddled up, and we headed down to the strike pad, where 15 CH-47 Chinook helicopters from the 159th Aviation Battalion were en route to pick up the entire battalion and transport us to the combat base at Quang Tri. While we assembled along the quarter-mile-long airstrip waiting to be assigned to a particular Chinook, our platoon leader came over to check everyone out and make sure we had all our gear. Roger informed us that we were headed for the DMZ, which was a bleak strip of no-man's land between North and South Vietnam. Our mission was to reinforce the 5th Mechanized Infantry Division, which had gotten into some heavy fighting with a large NVA unit. One of their small firebases had been overrun by the NVA and casualties were heavy. The 5th Mech used APCs (armored personnel carriers) and tanks to good advantage in the rolling, generally treeless terrain along the DMZ, but several more of their firebases were being threatened by elements of the 27th NVA Regiment. Rumors were rampant, and everyone was aware that we could be getting ourselves into some heavy fighting. After sitting on the pad talking and smoking for about an hour, we heard the big choppers coming. As they landed on the tarmac, we boarded quickly and belted in for the half-hour ride to the Quang Tri combat base. The Chinooks lifted off, almost in formation, and I could see familiar landmarks below as we flew north along the highway and across rice paddies and green fields. We were all nervous, aware of the heavy fighting that had taken place recently, and I prayed that we would all make it back safely. The flight was short, and after we landed at Quang Tri, the Chinooks lifted off again and headed back to their base in Phu Bai. They were too big to land on the small LZs we would be using on the DMZ and would have made great targets for the NVA gunners. Instead, the mission plans were to have us board Hueys for the combat assault into an area just south of the DMZ where NVA had been recently spotted. We assembled into our units and were told to chow down. Then the usual hurry-up-and-wait routine began as men checked their weapons, wrote letters, smoked cigarettes or just laid back and tried to catch a little rest while they could. Steve and I got into a spirited discussion about Dylan's latest song and tried not to think too much about the upcoming mission.

It was not too long before we heard the "whop, whop, whop" of approaching helicopters and saw a flight of Hueys from the 158th Aviation Battalion setting down on the tarmac. Bravo Company was on the first airlift, and we watched in silence as the choppers lifted off, circled and headed north toward the DMZ. Alpha Company was next. We boarded our choppers and lifted off, not knowing if the LZ was hot. About halfway to the LZ, Roger got a report from Bravo Company and he yelled, "Cold LZ!" Bravo had not received any hostile fire from the LZ when they landed, and that news caused all of us to breathe a silent sigh of relief.

During my tour in Vietnam, not many occasions were more nerve-wracking than a combat assault onto some LZ in the middle of the jungle. Often we did not know if the LZ was hot and we would be taking fire, or cold with no sign of the enemy. I think every man did some thinking about the possibility of a short future during the flight to an LZ. Hearing the words, "Going in hot!" and knowing the choppers were taking fire caused an inner feeling of raw fear and near nausea, accompanied by a huge adrenaline rush and a puckered rear end. There was a sense of inevitability as the realization hit that you had no control over the situation and your life was in the hands of fate.

I could see the LZ from the air as the choppers made their final approach and descent. It looked peaceful enough, but the pilots wanted to get in and out rapidly just in case things turned ugly. As we approached, the door gunners sprayed the treeline around the LZ with their M-60s just in case any enemy soldiers lurked there waiting for an opportunity to fire on the approaching helicopters. The choppers hovered about five feet above the ground because of stumps and other debris on the LZ, and we were literally kicked out by the door gunners, who were anxious to get the hell out of there as quickly as they could. When I jumped, I punctured the shin on my right leg with something sharp, possibly a thorn or sharp rock. It hurt but I did not have time to look at it, and my adrenaline was pumping so hard that all I could think of was to get off the LZ and into cover with the rest of the platoon.

After Alpha Company had been inserted onto the LZ, we moved out in a predetermined order. We didn't get too far before I began to smell the unmistakable stench of rotting corpses. Not far from the LZ we discovered several dead NVA soldiers scattered around a bunker complex that had been hit by artillery, probably the previous day. The bodies were bloated and pretty messed up, with hordes of flies buzzing all over them. They had been stripped of clothing and weapons and laid there rotting in the sun. During my entire tour in Vietnam I never got over the shock and horror of seeing dead bodies. It was damn sure nothing like the movies. As I made my way past these latest victims the smell made me gag, and I was reminded again of how fleeting life could be in this insane war.

It was late afternoon and we had only gone about a half-klick or so before we began setting up a consolidated position for the night with Bravo Company. We dug our foxholes and pulled C-rations out of our rucksacks, but it was hard to eat because the area had been previously occupied by ARVN (South Vietnamese) troops, and the combination of odors from the fishy-smelling Vietnamese nuoc mam sauce and human excrement nauseated me. Unlike American GIs, the ARVN troops were undisciplined and their campsites were a mess. They tossed their food cans and refuse everywhere and seemed to crap where they wanted. We always buried our trash and dug catholes for our latrine duties. After I had eaten a few crackers and some peaches, we continued to prepare for the coming night and set out claymores to cover the most likely routes of approach the NVA would take if they hit us. The puncture wound on my leg was beginning to hurt, but I did not pay too much attention to it with all the other activities that were occurring.

Just before it got dark, AK-47 fire erupted and I could see green enemy tracers whizzing over my head. We all hit the dirt and returned fire immediately with M-16s and our M-60 machine gun. A steady stream of red tracers zipped from our position toward the suspected NVA location. We did not know how large a force we had contacted but suspected it to be more than a squad. I lobbed about half a dozen HE rounds toward the suspected enemy position with my M-79 grenade launcher. The M-79 made the familiar "thump" sound as I fired, and I could hear the high explosive rounds land with a "ka-wump, ka-wump, ka-wump." I wondered if I had hit anyone.

About ten minutes later all the firing ceased abruptly and we watched nervously from our foxholes for any sign of enemy movement. Our foxhole was only about ten meters from some very thick elephant grass, and we were really nervous all night about sappers sneaking up close enough to lob grenades or satchel charges at us. A couple of Cobra gunships worked the suspected enemy position over with ARA (aerial rocket artillery) and miniguns just after it got dark, then headed back to Phu Bai. Two C-130s circled our position most of the night and dropped illumination flares. That helped us to see the perimeter fairly well, but the flickering light from the flares gave the landscape a ghostly and surreal look. Several times I thought I had seen something moving to our front, but it turned out to be nothing but my mind playing tricks on me. Everyone was jumpy and the captain set up two mad minutes, one at midnight and the other at 0300 hours. At the predetermined hour, we all opened up with our weapons and sprayed the vegetation surrounding our NDP. Fortunately we were not probed by sappers during the night and the morning finally came, much to everyone's relief.

After a hurried breakfast, we hoisted rucksacks heavy with extra ammo onto our backs and moved out to the west while Bravo Company headed north. Our progress was slow because we found a lot of evidence left by the NVA, including expended ammo, empty cans, and bloody bandages. By now my right leg was really starting to hurt. I noticed that it was beginning to swell, but there was nothing I could do but keep moving. Even though everyone was nervous and apprehensive about getting into a firefight, a certain whiff of adventure was in the air and it seemed to me that many men were looking forward to kicking some NVA ass.

We halted about noon to chow down, catch our breath and have a smoke. I had just finished eating when our platoon leader, Roger, came running over to where Steve and I were sitting. He was out of breath and told us the lookouts had spotted three or four NVA soldiers moving down a gully about 400 meters to our south. I grabbed my M-79 and bag of HE rounds while Steve and two other men grabbed M-16s, and we ran after the lieutenant toward the area where the lookouts had spotted the NVA. We crawled up a small rise through some elephant grass and carefully parted it to have a look at the gully.

Almost immediately, Roger and I spotted three NVA just as they disappeared into a small clump of brush in the gully. They had not spotted us, and the clump of brush was no more than 100 meters from us, so Roger told me to drop a couple of HE rounds on them. The grenade launcher made its familiar hollow "thump" as the HE round zipped toward the clump of brush where the NVA were hiding. The first round hit dead center with a loud "ka-wump" as it exploded. We had a pretty good view of the little clump of brush and did not see any movement or activity. I dropped two more rounds into the brush and they hit with a loud "ka-wump, ka-wump." Nobody came out. I was pretty sure the first round had either killed or mortally wounded the NVA soldiers, so we prepared to make a sweep of the area to check for bodies.

Just as we got ready to recon and check to see if we had killed the NVA, we got an urgent call on the radio instructing us to get back to the company perimeter ASAP. We had to abandon our plan to sweep the area to check for NVA bodies and returned to join the rest of the company.

We were told that an LOH pilot flying reconnaissance had spotted what he estimated to be at least a squad, maybe even a larger unit, of NVA soldiers holed up in a bunker complex. The bunkers were located at the junction of three large gullies about a klick east of our current position. We were told to leave our rucksacks where they were and to take only fighting gear and extra ammo. We planned to make a rapid advance and surround the NVA in the bunkers before they could get away. The 2nd Platoon stayed with the rucksacks and other gear while the 1st and 3rd Platoons headed for the bunker complex. We reached the area quickly, and the 3rd Platoon circled to occupy a ridge just east of the gully area where the bunkers had been spotted. The ridge was fairly open with some scattered trees, and we could see the men maneuver into position while we took positions on the west side of the bunker complex. Two Cobra gunships circled overhead and raked the bunkers with ARA and minigun fire. We could hear AK-47s firing back at the Cobras as we crawled toward the gullies about 50 meters ahead of our position. As soon as we got close enough to see the bunkers, we received intense AK-47 fire and several Chi Com grenades, or satchel charges, were lobbed up at us, but they fell short and did no damage. Billy, our machine gunner, finally got a good fix on the bunkers. He began to lay some heavy fire on them, but his gun jammed after a few minutes. After cussing a blue streak he finally cleared the weapon and continued to fire onto the bunkers while the rest of us opened up with everything we had. I fired my remaining HE rounds down into the bunker area, and after a couple of minutes we ceased fire. It was quiet so we thought we had neutralized the NVA troops, and we got on line to sweep the bunker complex. Very cautiously, we started down into the draw. All of a sudden, much to our amazement, the NVA opened up with their AKs. We returned fire to pin them down, but continued AK fire forced us to retreat back up the hill and take cover.

As we laid there trading fire with the NVA in the bunkers, we could see the 3rd Platoon on the ridge across from us. They could not see the bunkers from their position on the ridge unless they crawled forward. The two Cobra pilots that had been working the bunkers over with ARA and miniguns left for their base to refuel, and in a few minutes two new Cobras showed up to continue the bombardment. Then, very quickly, everything went terribly wrong.

Cobra gunship.

The new Cobra pilots evidently got confused or did not get correct information, because rather than continue to work over the gully area where the bunkers were located, they apparently mistook the 3rd Platoon on the ridge for the enemy and, as we watched in horror, began raking their position with ARA and minigun fire. We could see men trying to take what little cover there was and could hear them yelling and screaming. I saw several rockets hit, and the explosions threw several of the troopers into the air. By then we were all up and waving at the Cobras trying to get them to stop, but they probably mistook our gestures for cheers as they raked the hillside and ridgeline. Everything seemed to be a blur of slow motion, and someone was yelling, "If they don't stop, shoot them down!" Roger grabbed the radio from the RTO and after several attempts he made contact with the Cobra pilots. He screamed, "Cease fire! Cease fire, goddammit! You're killing friendlies!"

The Cobra pilots got the message and broke off the assault. We all waited in stunned silence while medevacs were called in to extract the wounded. From our vantage, it looked like at least six to ten men were being attended to by the medic and other soldiers from the 3rd Platoon. In about 20 minutes the medevac choppers arrived, and as they hovered above the ridge preparing to extract the wounded men, the NVA in the bunkers started to fire at the hovering medevacs. That was a clear violation of the Geneva Convention, and it outraged us. Roger directed us to maneuver and suppress the enemy fire, so we crawled toward the bunkers and hit the gooks with everything we had to keep them pinned down. It worked and the medevacs were able to safely extract all of the wounded soldiers.

After the medevacs left with the casualties, we were ordered to head for a nearby hill about a half-klick from the NVA bunker complex and set up our perimeter for the night. The firefight had lasted nearly three hours, and we were tired, hungry, thirsty, and most of all, disgusted and sick about what had just happened to the 3rd Platoon. As we made our way toward the NDP site I kept playing the events over and over in my head and wondering just how the hell things had gotten so screwed up. I realized, however, that in the fog of war not everything works as planned and things are not always as they appear. An honest, but tragic mistake had been made and some unlucky soldiers paid a heavy price. I just hoped and prayed that those men were not seriously wounded.

The 1st Platoon made it to the NDP site and began digging in, but we had only minimal food and water. We had left our rucksacks behind when we assaulted the bunker complex. A supply chopper brought in several cases of claymores and a few cases of C-rations which were divided among us, but that was it. After eating a pretty meager evening meal, we set out the claymores and prepared for what looked like a long night. Nerves were pretty frayed, but fortunately we did not get probed by the NVA during the night and I did manage to catch a little sleep. When I took my turn at guard duty that night I could not get the images of the 3rd Platoon getting hit by the Cobra gunships out of my mind, and the awful scene kept replaying over and over. I thought about how easily it could have been us and said a few extra prayers that night.

In the war movies I saw as a boy, things were always under control, everyone made the right moves, and there was very little visible blood. Real firefights were hardly like that. There was lots of noise, confusion, yelling and screaming, and sometimes lots of blood.

In many ways, the long nights that I spent peering from a foxhole in the jungle were the worst part of Vietnam for me. Sitting there gave me a lot of time to think, and all kinds of scenarios would run through my mind and my thoughts would run wild. Would I make it back home in one piece? Would I see my wife and family again? How would they react if I arrived in a metal coffin? Then I would snap back to reality, peer into the darkness, and listen for footsteps or a rustle in the grass or brush.

Early next morning, without eating any breakfast, we headed over to the bunker complex again and watched as Cobra gunships pounded the gully area again for about a half-hour before they returned to Quang Tri. A short time later the 2nd Platoon linked up with us, and everyone was happy to see that they were bringing our rucksacks with them. We began to collect our rucks, but after looking through the pile I could not find mine. I asked several men if they had seen my ruck, telling them exactly where I had left it, but nobody had seen it and it soon became apparent that my rucksack was lost and I would not see it again. I was almost out of ammo for my M-79 and had no food, so I had to beg a few HE rounds and some C-rations from the other men in the squad. That was not a big problem, but I was devastated because all of my personal effects were gone. All the letters from my wife that I had saved, the photos of her and my young son, my old Argus camera, my shaving kit, my cigarettes: all gone. It seemed that my only link to home had been severed. I felt bad but at the same time I was pissed off. How could this happen? Why was mine the only rucksack that was lost? Another screwup!

After a quick breakfast the 1st Platoon began to sweep down the gullies to check out the bunker complex, while the 2nd Platoon maneuvered around to form a blocking force. We did not encounter any resistance, and as we reached the area we saw three or four bunkers dug into the sides of the gullies. There were three dead NVA sprawled near the bunkers, evidently victims of the Cobra gunships because the bodies were full of holes and pretty messed up. We found a few mortar rounds, about a dozen RPGs, and an old SKS rifle. Besides the three NVA soldiers that had been killed, we had evidently wounded some others, because there were bloody bandages strewn around one of the bunkers. The wounded soldiers and their comrades had all escaped under the cover of darkness and had vanished into the night. It was amazing that anyone had lived through the Cobra bombardment, but the NVA were tough fighters and had learned how to survive. American air power had its limits.

Even though I hardly noticed it during all the commotion, my right leg had become painfully swollen and I was having a difficult time walking. Pus was oozing out of the wound and I was running a fever. Our medic took one look at my leg and told me he was putting me on the next supply chopper headed for Charlie Two, one of the 5th Mechanized Division's firebases, where there was a medical aid station. I did not argue with him because the pain had become intense and I knew I needed medical treatment. While we were eating lunch around noon, a chopper came in to resupply us and after the C-rations and ammo had been kicked out, I boarded and headed back to Charlie Two for medical attention. My time on the DMZ was over. I had mixed emotions about leaving the platoon before we had completed the mission, and I would miss my buddies. My leg was killing me, though, and I knew that it needed immediate treatment if I was to avoid losing it to a nasty infection.

As the Huey flew over the bombed and blasted landscape of the DMZ on its way back to Charlie Two, I watched the terrain pass by below us and had a few moments to reflect on the events of the last few days. Two events kept playing over and over in my head. I was still half in shock over seeing the 3rd Platoon getting ripped apart by the Cobra gunships. I also realized that I might have killed three NVA soldiers with my M-79, but since we did not have time to sweep the area, I would never know for certain. Maybe it was better that way.

When we landed on the helipad at Charlie Two, I hobbled over and reported to the Aid Station. Two orderlies cut off my right pants leg above the knee with a scissors to take a look at the wound, and it hurt like hell as they pulled the pus and blood-encrusted material away from my leg. A young doctor came over and asked me what had happened and I told him that I was not sure. He told me that I had a nasty infection in my leg and that he would have to drain it. With that he reached for a scalpel, and I remember saying "Oh no you don't!" as I backed away from him.

The doctor calmly said, "Grab him," to the two orderlies, and each one grabbed an arm and shoulder and held me down while the doctor reached down swiftly and lanced the wound with his scalpel. Then he grabbed my leg and squeezed it, trying to get all the pus out, and I nearly passed out from the pain. After he finished, my leg felt somewhat better, but I was weak and dizzy so they put me on a cot and gave me some Darvon and antibiotics. After the leg had drained for a while, the doctor washed the wound with antiseptic and packed the hole in my leg with a gauze "wick," he called it. I was assigned to a hootch and put on light duty, which meant I would be helping out in the mess tent. I actually did not mind it because I got to eat hot chow, and working in the kitchen peeling potatoes and washing pots and pans beat hell out of toting a rucksack in the boonies. I got to know a couple of guys who were stationed on Charlie Two, and we swapped stories about our units and where we had been in Vietnam.

I remained at Charlie Two for three days, and every day the doctor took the wick out of my leg, examined the wound, and swabbed it with antiseptic. By the third day the swelling had gone down and I was feeling much better, so I was released from the Aid Station. I hopped a log bird that was headed to the combat base in Quang Tri, and there I caught a Jeep that was driving south to Camp Sally. When I got back to Camp Sally I rejoined the rest of Alpha Company, all of whom had made it back safely from the DMZ. I found out that Alpha Company had been involved in a night assault along with tanks from the 5th Mech the same day that I had left for Charlie Two. They had been involved in an all-night battle with the NVA and had inflicted heavy casualties on the enemy. Everyone was excited about it, and the stories got better every day. In a way, I was sorry that I had missed out on all the action.

While we were back at Camp Sally, an awards formation was called and the battalion commander pinned a blue and silver CIB (Combat Infantryman Badge) on me for earlier actions with Alpha Company. Several other soldiers were also awarded CIBs at the ceremony. The CIB was one of the most coveted awards and it was issued only to infantry soldiers who had been in a firefight or had landed on a hot LZ. Of the various medals that I was eventually awarded for my service in Vietnam, I am most proud of my CIB.

Our operation near the DMZ resulted in 36 NVA killed, and we captured several heavy machine guns, AK-47s, a mortar tube, and assorted ammunition and other equipment. I never read anything about the friendly-fire incident involving the Cobra gunships and the 3rd Platoon in the military newspaper, *Stars and Stripes*, and nobody seemed to know exactly what had happened. It was surely not the kind of incident that got reported to the media in 1969. I do not believe that any of the men involved were killed, but I don't know that for certain. I never heard any more about the incident, and I guess I just wanted to forget the whole thing.

12

The Bridge

It did not seem much like Thanksgiving on hot and dusty Firebase Bastogne, but everyone looked forward to the turkey dinner we were promised. It didn't turn out half bad. The turkey, instant potatoes, dressing and other food was a huge improvement over the usual C-rations or lurps. Many of us had received care packages from our wives and folks back home, and whatever we received was shared with the other men in the squad. Candy, nuts, Kool-Aid and other sweet treats were always welcome. Somebody even sent me a large chunk of Wisconsin cheese, but it was not in the best shape after several weeks en route in the tropical heat. Many of the men requested that their folks send them cans of WD-40, which we used to clean and protect our weapons. It was not available from army supply, and the official LST oil was not always available either. I think most of all I liked getting letters and photos from home. I could not believe how little Timmy was growing, and Linda was growing too; she was pregnant with our second child. I missed all of them so much.

When I pulled my turn at guard duty that night, I looked up at a beautiful star-filled sky and was very thankful that I had survived for almost six months. I had a lot to reflect on; many things had happened in the short time I had been in Vietnam. My thoughts drifted to Linda, Tim, and the new baby on the way. I thought about my mom and dad and wished that I was home in Wisconsin getting ready for the annual deer hunt. My only hope was that the rest of my tour would pass quickly and smoothly so I could return home to the world.

Our short Thanksgiving stay on Bastogne went without major incident, and a few days later the 1st Platoon got new orders and boarded trucks for a short ride toward Hue. Nobody seemed to know what was going on and if they did, they were not saying anything. The trucks lumbered northeast for several klicks and dropped us off at Pohl Bridge, also known as the Nam Hoa Bridge. We had drawn some primo duty, as the lieutenant put it, and we were more than happy to spend a week in a location that seemed idyllic compared to the places we had been recently. The concrete bridge spanned the Song Huu Trach about eight klicks south of Hue on Route 547. The small village of Nam Hoa was 1.5 klicks to the southeast of the bridge, and many Vietnamese hootches were scattered nearby along the road. The bridge was a vital link between Hue and the firebases to the west and was a potential target for sabotage by NVA sappers or Viet Cong guerrillas.

Large sandbagged bunkers guarded both approaches to the bridge, and another bunker sat along a dirt road that paralleled the river. A small navy compound was situated along the river. It had its own guard bunker, and there were several antennas protruding from the roof of the main building. We found out that the compound was a freshwater pumping station for Hue, manned by the Seabees. The bridge itself was a concrete structure about 100 meters long and 10 or 15 meters high. Our mission was to secure the bridge at night and make certain that nobody tried to blow it up. Besides being on constant alert at each bunker, we patrolled in pairs back and forth on the bridge at night, occasionally dropping concussion or fragmentation grenades over the side in case anyone was trying to plant explosives under the bridge. It was fun to drop the grenades over the side and listen to them explode with a loud "ka-woom!"

During the day we spent time swimming in the river and playing catch with an old football we got from the Seabees. The river was deep and cool and felt really refreshing in the tropical heat. If it were not for the guards posted up and downstream from where we were swimming, one could easily have imagined that he was swimming in a river back in Georgia or Wisconsin. Most of us did a lot of reading, and I remember reading a book of poems by Walt Whitman and enjoying it a lot. It was also a great chance to catch up on letter writing. We talked with the local inhabitants of the village, mostly the kids. The week turned out to be pretty laid back, and everyone was able to relax and get a little rest.

Pohl Bridge, near village of Nam Hoa.

Village of Nam Hoa.

The local Vietnamese went about their daily business of farming, gardening, and fishing in the river. Old men tended their water buffalo and hauled wood and straw on carts to the village. The women went about doing laundry in the river, beating clothes on rocks and spreading them out in the sun to dry. Some of them even offered to wash our backs when we went to the river to swim. The younger women wore colorful ao dais, which were long dresses or tunics that were worn over long silk pants. Most of the older women chewed betel nuts, which were a mildly euphoric stimulant. The red juice often ran out of the corners of their mouths, and the long-term use of betel nuts turned their teeth coal-black. It was not an attractive look to most westerners. The people in the village were very friendly and we bartered with them for fresh vegetables and fruit in exchange for C-rations.

Most of the kids spoke understandable English, and we had fun kidding with them and trading stories. They also begged for C-rations every day and got much of our supply since we had hot chow trucked in to us once a day. One of the older boys, who was probably about 13 years old, was a real hustler and constantly tried to sell us things. He had about 20 watches on his arm, including several "genuine Rolex" that he was willing to sell for a mere $5.00 American. Everybody called him "Slicky Boy," but I doubt he made too many watch sales. I took a particular liking to cute little girl about four or five years old, and I gave her candy or gum every day. She always smiled and laughed, then said something in Vietnamese that I did not understand, and ran to the village.

After a few days I became curious and asked Slicky Boy what the little girl was saying to me. He simply laughed and said, "She says, 'Fuck you,' GI."

The little girl obviously did not understand what she said or what it meant, but the incident was a sad testament to the loss of innocence of a whole generation of people in Vietnam. Many of the young children smoked cigarettes and acted as pimps for their older sisters or their mothers. Another sad result of war, I thought, but like most of us my primary focus was on my own survival, not what was happening to the Vietnamese people.

Outskirts of Hue.

One day when I had guard duty on the bridge a small convoy of ROK (Republic of Korea) troops drove past me. They had a strange, fierce appearance to me, but they seemed friendly and waved to me as they began to cross the bridge. I was shocked to discover that they had roped the naked corpse of an NVA or VC soldier they had killed onto the back of one of the Jeeps. The display was no doubt meant to send a message to any Viet Cong sympathizers in the area. The ROK troops had the reputation of being fierce fighters who had no sympathy for enemy troops. Apparently the reputation was well-deserved.

Most U.S. troops, including our company, had a fairly negative opinion of ARVN soldiers and we considered most of them to be lazy and incompetent. South Vietnamese army training was relatively poor by our standards, and many officers gained their rank based more on their wealth and political standing than on their military knowledge and skill. In many instances it seemed to us that the ARVN soldiers went out of their way to avoid contact with the enemy. We derogatorily referred to them as "cowboys." However, some ARVN troops were very good, including the 1st ARVN Division.

The week we spent guarding the bridge near Hue turned out to be one of the most enjoyable missions I can remember. Besides being able to swim, relax, and take it easy, the opportunity to learn a little more about the Vietnamese culture was very rewarding. Most of the people were Buddhists, but there were also some Roman Catholics. I had seen the large Catholic cathedral in Hue when we had driven through in a convoy several weeks earlier. We had also learned how the Vietnamese made their awful-smelling nuoc mam sauce. Fish heads were put into a cloth bag and hung in the sun to ferment. As the fish rotted the juices dripped into a jar. They added some other ingredients, I think, but it didn't matter; the whole concoction stank to high heaven! When we got orders to return to Bastogne the following week, everyone really hated to leave the bridge.

After two days on Bastogne doing little more than stringing wire and filling sandbags, we were told to grab our gear and head to the helipad. Nobody knew what was up, but finally the lieutenant was told that we were going north to Camp Evans to do some patrolling in the low hills around the base. Camp Evans was a large 101st Airborne Division base along Highway 1, several klicks northwest of Camp Sally. The Hueys set down on the helipad and Alpha Company boarded them for the short flight to Evans. There had been some NVA activity near the firebase, and we planned to patrol for a few days to see if we could interrupt the activity. We all sat near the helipad and chowed down for lunch, then prepared to move out. The 1st Platoon had the northwest sector of the base to patrol, and we headed for a range of low hills about a half-klick away. I was surprised because there was not much cover, just a lot of brush. There were a lot of gullies that wound through the hills, and these gave a certain amount of cover, particularly at night. After about two hours of moving through the dissected terrain, we stopped for a break on a low hill and put security out on all sides. We had no more than lit up a cigarette when Manny and James opened up with their M-16s. They quit after each had emptied a clip of ammo, and Roger ran over to see what was happening. They reported that they had seen two Vietnamese men running down a gully about 75 meters from them and it appeared that they each had a weapon. They were not uniformed NVA regulars, and Roger reported them as local VC soldiers whom we had surprised. When Roger asked Manny if they had hit anything, Manny replied in his usual drawl, "Nah, them gooks was haulin' ass and all we did was scare the shit out of 'em."

Two more days of meandering around the hills did not yield any more sightings of NVA or VC, and in fact there was very little evidence that the area was being used at all. It turned out to be a fairly easy mission, and since we were so close to Camp Evans, we had hot chow flown out to us every evening. On the third day we headed back to the base and hit the showers to wash the dust and dirt away and cool off. After some great chow in a huge mess hall, we bunked down in a tent and were happy that we did not have to pull guard duty that night. Most of the men headed to the EM club and drank themselves into oblivion before they returned to our tent and crashed for the night. The next day we headed to the helipad and waited for several hours before some Hueys choppered us back to Firebase Bastogne again.

About mid–December the 1st Platoon drew some more laid-back duty after we had spent a week in the boonies, patrolling without making any contact with the NVA. We got assigned to provide security at the Hue Ramp, which was a small navy Seabees compound in the middle of Hue

Farmers with water buffalo near Camp Evans.

on the Perfume River. The compound was surrounded by a 10-foot chain-link fence and several rows of barbed and concertina wire. Large sand-bagged bunkers were located beside the gates at each end of the compound. We took turns pulling guard duty in the bunkers, but most of the day and night was pretty much R&R for us. We had a barracks with cots to sleep on, and a very nice mess hall served wonderful food, unlike anything we had eaten in army mess halls. Again, we caught up on our letter writing, read books, and played cards. A movie was shown in the mess hall every night, and everyone not on guard duty usually attended.

We all thought, "These navy guys know how to live" and envied them for the plush lifestyle they enjoyed compared to the grungy existence of the average infantry soldier. During the day, some troops were given permission to go into Hue. I made one trip with Greg and several other buddies into the city, where we picked up souvenirs and took photos of the people and the city. Hue was bustling with activity, and people on motor-bikes and bicycles were everywhere. The market was crowded with food and junky souvenirs, and we had fun bartering with the merchants. It was

Ancient Imperial city of Hue.

Small children near Hue.

hard to imagine that the city had been decimated just a year earlier during the Tet Offensive. Kids were everywhere, selling the usual selection of items including trinkets, cold sodas, dope, and their older sisters. One older woman, maybe about 35, approached us and grabbed Greg's hand, trying to lead him into a nearby hootch. It was obvious what she was selling, but nobody wanted any part of that because we had been warned about the high rate of VD in the city. Besides, the woman was about as ugly as any I had ever seen, and Greg just kept laughing as she became more desperate. Finally, Greg shook her off and we went on our way. Greg laughed some more and said, "I believe that if I would have hung around for another minute, she would have offered to pay me." After a while the hustle got to all of us and we headed back to the compound for evening chow and a movie.

After about three days at the navy compound, I began to feel sick and initially thought that it was due to all the good navy food. I was eating far more than I usually did in the field, and I had been drinking beer every night. It didn't take long, however, before I had uncontrollable diarrhea and a high temperature. Between trips back and forth to the latrine, I was burning up with fever and my eyes felt like hot coals. Then I got the chills and laid on my cot covered with a wool blanket, trying to keep warm in the tropical heat.

The medic looked at me and talked with the new platoon leader. They both questioned me and asked if I had been taking my malaria pills. I told them that I had, though many of us did not take them regularly, and it became apparent that they thought I was coming down with malaria. They talked about sending me to Phu Bai, but I told them I was beginning to feel better so they let me stay and gave me some pills to take. Besides, I had been one of three men from the platoon chosen to attend the Bob Hope Christmas show at Camp Eagle, and there was no way in hell that I was going to miss my chance to see the show. Given the symptoms that I had, I now believe that I either did have a slight case of malaria or more likely a case of dengue fever, but I will never know for certain. I gradually felt a little better, but the fever hung on and I alternated between feeling sick and feeling well. After a week, our mission in Hue was over and we boarded trucks and rode back to Camp Sally for Christmas standdown.

On Christmas Eve I attended mass in the base chapel. Things seemed to be almost like any service at home, but then the chaplain made remarks about how God was on our side and how he would protect us from the enemy. I had not gone to mass to hear an army propaganda speech, and the whole episode turned me off. I wondered if the NVA had God on their side too. In spite of that, I did go to mass a couple of times later on in the field. There were occasions when we were in a relatively safe area and a chaplain came out to the field to say mass for us. Most of the men attended, whether or not they were Catholic. I think it was a tie to home that made everyone feel some hope.

After a hearty breakfast on December 25, I boarded a Jeep with the two other soldiers I did not know, and we headed to Camp Eagle to see the Bob Hope Christmas show. I was still fairly sick and had a fever, but I was excited and there was no way I wanted to miss seeing Bob Hope. We arrived at Camp Eagle along with about 16,000 other eager GIs to see the man who had done so much for the military for so many years. I was about 150 feet from the stage, so I got a pretty good view. The two-hour show got started after we waited in the hot sun for about an hour. Astronaut Neil Armstrong, who had been on the moon in July, was there, along with Connie Stevens, Theresa Graves, the Golddiggers, and Miss World. Les Brown and his orchestra provided music, and everyone absorbed every minute of the show, which was a memorable event in the midst of an otherwise insane year. After the show I headed back to Camp Sally and was put on sick leave for a couple of days. Gradually I began to get my strength back and feel better, so I knew I would be heading back to the field soon.

I rejoined the platoon a day or two later, and we spent the rest of December on Firebase Bastogne, pulling guard duty at night and patrolling the surrounding jungle during the day. Nothing much happened and the patrols became extremely boring. The captain was concerned that everyone was getting complacent because of the lull, so he had us practicing live-fire bunker assaults on some old bunkers just outside the firebase perimeter. At night, my squad was assigned to a bunker that was directly below a 175mm howitzer battery on the south side of the firebase. That turned out to be more than just an annoyance. When they fired the big guns, the concussion nearly burst our eardrums — it was actually painful. One of the men's ears began to bleed, but all the medics did was give him cotton to stuff into his ears. The latest scuttlebutt making the rounds was that the base was going to be attacked on New Year's Eve. Just how that was known was a mystery to me, but everyone was on full alert that night. Several mad minutes were scheduled throughout the night, but the base was not probed or attacked and nothing happened. Rumors were part of daily life, and it seemed that more often than not, whatever was rumored never happened. The unexpected seemed to occur just when everyone thought that everything was under control and going well.

Things started to heat up a little in the middle of January, when Bravo Company found about a dozen booby traps made with 60mm mortar rounds. The 1st Battalion discovered and destroyed 17 NVA bunkers just west of Hue and found more booby traps. The 3rd Battalion got into a firefight with some enemy soldiers and ended up killing nine of them. A few days later, while Alpha Company was on a mission about 40 klicks southwest of Hue, we were moving along a fairly large trail in triple-canopy jungle when we began to take fire from an enemy force of unknown size. After the first volley of AK-47 fire, everyone hit the dirt and returned fire. Miraculously, nobody had been hit, and after that first volley, the NVA quit firing. They had either left the area or holed up in bunkers. The captain calculated the probable enemy coordinates, and our RTO called on the radio and requested a fire mission. Within 15 minutes Cobra gunships appeared in the sky and came in, raking the area with ARA (aerial rocket artillery) and mini-gun fire. After about an hour, we swept the area and found two well-hidden bunkers and three dead NVA soldiers. We took their weapons and other supplies, then checked for any documents but didn't find any. The rest of the hostile forces, however many there had been, evaporated into the surrounding jungle. It seemed that the enemy was up to something. All three platoons in Alpha Company, as well as Bravo and Charlie Companies, were running into enemy contact fairly frequently, and we were finding caches of weapons and ammo and numerous small bunker complexes. Luckily, nobody in Alpha Company was wounded or killed.

During this time period a new captain assumed command of Alpha Company. He was a pleasant, competent commanding officer and I immediately liked him. His concern for the men was evident and he did what he could to make life bearable for us. One day after I had volunteered to walk point, he called me over and told me that no married man with a family was going to walk point in his company. Like most men, I did not like to walk point but felt that some of the cherries were not experienced enough to keep us out of trouble. My life should not have been any more valuable than the life of a single man. I did not argue with the captain, however, and I felt a sense of relief. I convinced myself that after eight months in the field I had probably walked point enough. I wondered if I was beginning to lose my edge and thought that maybe it was time for my luck to run out. Maybe, as the captain had said, I was getting a little too comfortable and complacent.

Greg, Larry, and I had been in the field about eight months. One day while reading the *Stars and Stripes* military newspaper that came with the resupply, we saw an article indicating that several 101st Airborne Division helicopter units were looking for door gunners. Door gunners were the crew members on Huey and Chinook helicopters who manned the M-60 machine guns. It was probably one of the more dangerous jobs in Vietnam, and we were aware that helicopters were often fired on more frequently than were troops on the ground. However, the thought of eating hot chow every day and sleeping in a bunk was too much to resist after having spent eight months living under miserable field conditions. After some discussion, all three of us asked the company commander for permission to apply for transfers to be door gunners. Surprisingly, he agreed, and we submitted our requests for transfer immediately, before he changed his mind.

Toward the end of January we were at Camp Sally for a brief stand-down. A few days later, on February 4, I got called into the company clerk's office and was told that the company commander had been informed by the Red Cross that my wife had given birth to our second son, Joseph. At first I was kind of numb. After all the time in the field, I was not accustomed to thinking about home as much as I had earlier during my tour. After the news sank in, I was overwhelmed with happiness and vowed to myself that I was going to return home no matter what happened and that nothing would stand in my way. The birth of my second son was all the excuse that Larry, Greg, and I needed for a big celebration at the EM club that night.

13

Door Gunner

I could not believe my luck when I found out a few days later that my request for a transfer went through. Greg and I would be going to Alpha Company in the 159th Aviation Battalion, an outfit that flew Chinook helicopters. Their call sign was "Pachyderms" and the compound was near Phu Bai. Larry had also received orders and would be just up the road with Charlie Company in the 158th Aviation Battalion, which flew UH-1 Hueys. My days with the infantry were almost over, and I looked forward to getting out of the field in a week and flying on a CH-47 Chinook. Most of my infantry company buddies were fairly new, and I had not formed strong bonds with any of them except for Steve. He was probably my best friend and I would miss him and our long discussions about Bob Dylan, but it was time for me to move on.

The day we reported for duty with the 159th Aviation Battalion in Phu Bai must have been a spectacle for the troops who were stationed there. We were dressed in our ragged, dirty jungle fatigues, and we got some disdainful looks from the other troops. The first thing we did was to hit the mess hall, which was unlike anything we had experienced on the firebases. The quality and variety of food was amazing to us, and we tried to eat everything in sight. It was difficult for us to realize that we were actually out of the bush and would be living the good life in comparison to the life we had just left. The compound that the 159th occupied was situated near Phu Bai and surrounded by villages and farms. The ground was mostly white sand, similar to what we had seen at Eagle Beach, and there were boardwalks constructed everywhere that led from

2nd Platoon's hootch on Phu Bai compound.

one building to another. It was easier walking on them than it was in the loose sand.

Next we got assigned to our new flight platoons: Greg went to the 1st Platoon and I was assigned to the 2nd Platoon. The supply clerk issued us new fatigues, Nomex suits, leather boots, and a flight helmet. Then we were taken to our flight platoon hootches, which were plush compared to the bunkers we had called home on Bastogne and Birmingham. I began to meet the men in the platoon, and most of them were young and not much different from those I had left behind in my infantry unit. There were a few older guys like myself and some college graduates, including the officers and warrant officers. I noticed right away that none of the men had the distant stare and hardened look that was so obvious in many of the infantry grunts. My area in the hootch was a small section with a foot locker, wall locker and stacked bunks. A big screened window near my bunk faced a large sandbagged bunker that was located along the side of the hootch. I met my new roommate, a guy from Wisconsin named Eddie. His friends Chuck and Rick came by and said hello when I was stowing my gear in the wall locker.

They all seemed like nice guys, and I noticed right away that they were sporting mustaches, something that had been strictly forbidden in my old infantry unit. My new buddies seemed like colorful characters, dressed in their Hawaiian shirts and headbands. They reminded me of hippies who had been pressed into military service, but I found out later that all of them were enlistees, not draftees like me. They tried to make me feel at home and wanted to know what it was like to be a grunt. I did not have much to say about the bush, and it didn't take me long to settle into the routine and get comfortable with the laid-back lifestyle. I was excited when I got assigned as gunner aboard Pachyderm 532 because Eddie was the crew chief on that aircraft. I began growing a mustache immediately because I wanted to fit in with the rest of my new unit, and I thought it would give me a jaunty look.

There were two other flight platoons, and their hootches were next to ours. The officers' quarters sat off by themselves about 50 meters from our hootches, and there was a large wooden latrine about 30 meters from our hootch. The mess hall and weapons hootch sat on the other end of the compound, and there was a large open area in the center that had a stage and large movie screen just to the side of it. On one end of the compound there was a large metal hangar and a protected area where all of the company's Chinook helicopter were parked. The motor pool and EM club were on the other side of the compound.

After Greg and I had made pigs of ourselves in the mess hall and stowed our gear in our new hootches, we grabbed towels and headed for the shower room, which was just behind the hootches. The room was large and the cement floor felt cool on our feet as we stripped and turned on the showers. Before we knew it, there were two middle-aged women in the shower with soap in their hands, and they began to scrub our backs. Greg was so surprised that he exclaimed loudly, "What the hell is going on here?" The women kept repeating, "Wash back, wash back." As we found out later, it was apparently the custom of the Vietnamese hootch maids to scrub the backs of the soldiers in the shower room, and the women considered it part of their job. They also did our laundry every few days, but after a week or two it was obvious that socks and other clothing often disappeared and never returned. I never said anything because the people were very poor and did what they could to survive. The U.S. Army was a treasure trove to them.

Hootch maid on Phu Bai compound.

There were other local villagers who fought over the right to gather food and other material from the base dump. I watched one day as they filtered through our garbage, taking anything that was salvageable and putting it in their little carts. I watched one old man gathering what was left of some lettuce and other produce that had been discarded by the mess

Author in Nomex flight suit, Phu Bai compound.

hall. To these poor people, we were a valuable resource and I suspect that we supplied them with a significant amount of food. It was humbling and shameful to watch these people act like scavengers just to live. I felt sorry for them, but there was very little that I could do.

A Chinook helicopter crew consisted of a pilot, co-pilot, flight engineer, crew chief, and door gunner. The Nomex flight suit, leather boots and flight helmet that had been issued to us served a specific purpose aboard our aircraft. The helmet had a microphone and a cord that plugged in and connected us to the aircraft's radio so we could communicate with the pilot and other crew members. The flight helmet that I got had been decorated by the previous user. It had some flowers painted on the back with the words, "Blood, Sweat, and Tears." I liked that display and thought it was kind of a counterculture comment about the war. Surprisingly, nobody ever said anything about my helmet with its unauthorized artwork. Nomex was a flame-retardant fabric worn because of the fire danger if an aircraft crashed. We also wore leather boots rather than the nylon-shanked jungle boots for the same reason. While we were flying we wore a vest that contained a kevlar panel in the front. Everyone called them "chicken plates." They were heavy and uncomfortable, but they supposedly would stop an AK-47 round. Thankfully, I never had to find out.

We flew almost every day and normally started our flight prep after a predawn breakfast. Before every flight I helped the crew chief and flight engineer check and prep the aircraft and installed the M-60 machine guns in the door openings. After filling a large Igloo cooler with ice water and making sure that we had extra C-rations on board, we were ready for the day's mission. We usually began our flight operations just before the sun came up and on most days did not return to the base until dark. My major duties were providing security with the M-60 machine gun and advising the pilots of approaching air traffic or other conditions that could affect the aircraft. Quite often, when hovering over a firebase or landing with troops, our rotors came very close to trees or other obstacles, and it was extremely important to keep the pilots advised because their peripheral vision was limited. If our rotor blades were to strike any trees or rocks the blades would rapidly disintegrate and the helicopter would spin out of control and crash. Crew survival then depended on how quickly the fuel ignited and how fast they could get out of the wreckage.

Eddie told me about a guy who had been in the platoon a few months before I arrived. He had been, as Eddie put it, "a real loser and stupid to boot." The guy apparently did not have any depth perception, a critical skill if one was to watch for rotor blades getting too close to trees or other obstacles. He had almost allowed Eddie's aircraft to get too close to some trees near a firebase, and the rotors had clipped some small branches. Had the ship gone down in that location, it would have been disastrous because the hill was steep and covered with large rocks. After they returned to Phu Bai, Eddie had talked to the platoon sergeant and had the guy removed from the flight platoon and assigned to the mess hall.

The Chinook was capable of lifting heavy loads, and most of our missions involved hauling supplies into firebases. The supplies included ammunition, C-rations, howitzers, and large rubber bladders called blivets that contained drinking water or fuel. Occasionally we transported troops between larger firebases and other rear areas. The "bus run," which was air service between Phu Bai and Da Nang, was one of my favorite flight operations. That particular mission involved picking up troops in Phu Bai and transporting them to Da Nang. It was a beautiful one-hour flight along the coast of the South China Sea down to Marble Mountain in Da Nang. The scenery along the coastline was beautiful and it took my mind off of Vietnam, at least for a while. We usually flew over a small fishing village on our way to Da Nang, and occasionally we could see people waving at us. Boats were everywhere and I tried to imagine what it would be like to live and work there every day. We usually stayed in DaNang for several hours, which allowed us time to shop at a large PX and get our fill of hamburgers and french fries for lunch.

I absolutely loved the feeling of flying in the big, powerful Chinooks, listening to the whine of the engines and the thump of the rotors as the aircraft floated in the thick air just above the verdant landscape. Nothing compared to the thrill I got when we skimmed along, barely above tree-top level, in the cool early morning air as we crossed rice paddies and villages on our flight toward the distant purple mountains to the west. One of the pilots I flew with occasionally took delight in flying very low to the ground, barely clearing villages and farmers working in their fields. On one occasion he hovered over a dump, and the rotor wash blew debris all over the poor people who were foraging in the dump for food and other items. None of us on board thought much of these antics, nor did we like the pilot. As one of the crew put it, "He's nothing but an asshole with wings." Most of the time I felt both safe and invincible in the air, although I certainly understood the risks of flying in the big twin-rotor birds. There were many things that could easily go wrong mechanically, and there was the constant threat of being shot out of the sky by enemy machine gun or anti-aircraft fire.

Our missions took us all over I Corps, from Quang Tri, below the DMZ, south to Da Nang and west to the many firebases in and near the dreaded Ashau Valley. Shortly after I joined the Pachyderms, we flew near the abandoned marine firebase at Khe Sahn and our pilot decided to land and check things out. We got out to look around, but the idea quickly turned sour when our flight engineer mentioned that booby traps or unexploded mortar rounds were likely still there. I had a very eerie feeling as I looked at the surrounding hills and mountains, trying to visualize the siege that had taken place there not long ago. I was convinced that the

Fishing village on South China Sea, between Hue and Da Nang.

Chinook flying over rice paddies.

ghosts of the dead still hovered around the base. With that, we boarded
and took off because we did not want to remain long enough to draw
enemy fire.

We spent most of February resupplying Firebases Fuller, Barbara,
Mooney, and others that I don't recall. Within that month one of our aircraft was hit by enemy fire but returned to base safely. Toward the end of
February, hostilities started to increase, and flying supplies into the string
of firebases between Hue and the Ashau Valley became increasingly dangerous. We started to receive small-arms fire on a regular basis, and several aircraft were hit but did not sustain any serious damage. Many of us
thought the increased fire we were receiving was a direct result of the Nixon

Vietnamization policy, which encouraged the South Vietnamese to take more responsibility for fighting the war. The ARVN troops simply did not pursue the NVA as aggressively as did the Americans. Consequently, many of the firebases were surrounded by NVA troops and anti-aircraft emplacements. In March we moved a howitzer battery to Firebase O'Reilly and inserted troops and equipment onto Firebase Granite. A few weeks later Granite came under heavy ground attack, and scores of NVA were killed as they stormed the base. I was on Pachyderm 532 the next morning with Eddie. We flew to resupply the base with ammo and to remove several cargo nets full of dead NVA soldiers and body parts.

Later that same day we hovered near the refueling station on the edge of Camp Evans and waited as the crew on Pachyderm 535 refueled. Just as the aircraft started to lift off, it suddenly crashed back to earth from about 10 feet and immediately burst into a ball of fire. The aircraft apparently had been overloaded and the engines overstressed. I felt sick as we quickly circled and landed nearby. I knew the crew and was certain I had just witnessed them all being burned to death. After we landed, however, we found out that the crew had miraculously escaped, but there were several passengers injured and a trooper from one of the infantry companies had been killed.

A mission to deliver a large blivet of water to one of the remote firebases almost turned to tragedy one hot afternoon about a week after 535 crashed. As we hovered, trying to place the load where the men on the ground wanted it, we started to lose altitude in the thin mountain air. To avoid crashing, the flight engineer punched the load off from about 20 feet and the blivet went hurtling to the ground and burst, spilling all of the water. As we circled the base, we were stunned when the flight engineer announced on the radio that from his vantage point it appeared we had just crushed a bunch of men with the blivet. A short time later, however, we got a call from the base informing us that the blivet had somehow missed the men and nobody was hurt. We all breathed a big sigh of relief as we headed to get another blivet to replace the one that was destroyed.

A few days later an unusual mission had us dropping a large blivet full of jet fuel onto an abandoned NVA bunker complex that was discovered by an infantry platoon. We flew two klicks south of Firebase

Bastogne and checked the area for any signs of enemy movement. The bunkers appeared to be deserted, so we hovered and punched the load off. The blivet burst when it hit the ground, spilling fuel all over the bunkers. Then the flight engineer dropped a white phosphorus grenade down on the fuel-soaked bunkers and the whole complex went up in flames. Anyone hiding in the bunkers would have been roasted alive.

Several firebases in the Ashau Valley area were hit by the NVA during March, and we continued to resupply them with food and ammunition. On at least two missions we extracted the bodies of NVA soldiers who had been killed trying to penetrate the firebase perimeter defenses. The bodies were piled into a cargo net, and we simply hooked onto the net and carried them back to Camp Sally or Camp Evans. After we deposited them, presumably to be searched for documents and then buried in a mass grave, onlookers gathered to ogle and take pictures. I could never understand how anyone could take pleasure in viewing dead human beings. Most of the viewers were no doubt rear-eschelon soldiers who had never ventured beyond the perimeter of the base camp. I guess this was their "moment of glory." I hated these missions. Viewing and smelling mangled, dead bodies was sickening and it disgusted me, even though they were enemy soldiers.

In late March or early April, Firebases O'Reilly, Fuller, Sarge, and Granite had been socked in by heavy fog for almost two weeks and were running dangerously low on supplies and ammunition. We finally resupplied the bases by hovering at treetop level and flying slowly up the steep mountain slopes to the bases on top. I was not that worried about taking ground fire but thought several times during the mission that we would hit trees with our rotors and crash. Luckily, no aircraft were lost.

In April the battalion attempted to insert at Firebase Ripcord, but the LZ was hot and a UH-1 Huey was shot down. Incoming mortar rounds, RPGs, and .51 caliber machine-gun fire prevented the insertion of the troops. (For a detailed account of Firebase Ripcord and the events leading up to the time it was overrun by the NVA, see the book *Ripcord: Screaming Eagles Under Siege, Vietnam 1970* by Keith W. Nolan.) A few weeks later one of the Chinooks from Bravo Company took heavy enemy fire when it approached Firebase Fuller and was shot down. It seemed as though the NVA had decided to challenge our presence in the mountains west of Hue, and flying was getting very dangerous.

Back at the compound in Phu Bai, everything was pretty relaxed compared to the way it had been in the boonies or on the firebases. For the most part, life was good. The food was tasty and plentiful, and we often had steaks and ice cream, something that was pretty unusual for infantry platoons. A movie was shown just about every night except when it rained. Every few weeks we were treated to a performance by a touring USO show. Most of the entertainers were not that good, but nobody cared because any kind of entertainment was a welcome relief from the daily boredom and many of the men were drunk or stoned anyway. There was a lot of drinking in the EM club every night, and there was no shortage of beer. About half of the troops smoked marijuana on a regular basis at night, but I never saw or heard of anybody smoking dope while they were on duty. It did not seem to get out of hand, and I never knew of anyone who did hard drugs. Occasionally we had to pull bunker guard duty, but compared to bunker guard on forward firebases, it was a cakewalk. The mess hall even brought sandwiches and hot coffee to the bunkers around midnight. On one occasion, I was making the rounds, inspecting bunkers. As I entered one of the bunkers a young Vietnamese hooker appeared from inside. The troops in the bunker did not seem to realize that allowing non-military personnel like that inside our compound at night put all of us at risk. After a good ass-chewing, I told them to send the hooker out the way she came in and to not let me catch her in the bunker again.

I did not observe very much overt racism in any of the flight platoons except for some occasional mocking or taunting. There was one white soldier who thought it was funny to make fun of the "dap" that the black soldiers used as a greeting. That is, until he did it once too often and got knocked onto his ass by a very big black soldier. There was one incident that could have turned tragic if it had been allowed to escalate. I had just returned from a flight and was taking my guns into the armory for cleaning when I accidentally bumped a black soldier who was also entering the building. He took the bump as a deliberate racist challenge, and I found myself staring at the business end of an M-60 being held by a pissed-off door gunner. I apologized, and after the situation calmed down we shook hands and went our separate ways. Some of my buddies urged me to report the incident, but I did not feel the need to do so; the black soldier and I had come to an understanding and the event was over as far as I was concerned.

Life in a rear area was very different from that in the bush with an infantry unit. One evening just after chow, the local Viet Cong dropped one mortar round onto the fuel dump and hit a diesel storage tank, setting off a huge blaze. As the black smoke billowed toward the sky, men were running around with weapons and looking for places to hide. Greg and I didn't get too concerned. We had experienced mortar fire before and knew this was an isolated event. The difference between rear-area troops and those in infantry units was very obvious to us.

One "good ole boy" from Tennessee received a bottle of bourbon from his wife every month. The scenario that followed was very predictable, and several of us enjoyed watching it unfold. Lester would get homesick, feel sorry for himself, and by the time he was totally drunk he would get pugnacious and start turning over wall lockers and punching walls. The next day he was just Lester again.

One potentially deadly incident of "fragging" occurred during a movie one night. As we watched the movie, there was a loud "ka-boom" and we saw the first sergeant's hootch explode. Luckily, he was watching the movie with us and nobody was injured. As it turned out, a soldier who worked in the motor pool was disgruntled about something the first sergeant had done and had tossed a concussion grenade under the hootch. The next day I watched as the MPs (military police) led the man away in handcuffs. I never heard what happened to him, but I suspect that he went to the stockade in Long Binh.

When I heard about a program that would allow me to leave the military about five months early, I jumped at the chance to sign up. I found out that if I was enrolled to attend college after I returned to the United States, I could get an early discharge from the army. Since I did not want to spend five months on some base back in the United States, I arranged for Linda to enroll me for the fall semester at my alma mater in Stevens Point, and I signed the papers for my early out. To qualify for the program, I had to extend my tour of duty in Vietnam, so instead of leaving in May, I would now be leaving in July. That was probably not the smartest move I ever made, and little did I know just how much risk I was undertaking with my decision to stay in Vietnam for another two months.

14

Getting Short

In late April I was finally scheduled to go on my R&R to Hawaii. Because of the heavy demand, only married men were usually allowed to go to Hawaii to meet their wives. There were also R&R locations in Bangkok, Tokyo, Singapore, Manila, Taipei, and Kuala Lumpur. All of these places were very popular with the single guys.

I caught a bus run flight to Da Nang and reported to the R&R center, where I spent the night. The following morning after breakfast I received instructions for the trip to Hawaii, along with several other men who were also anxious to see their wives. All of us received shaving kits from the Red Cross, which I thought was kind of strange. Then we boarded a C-130 that was headed for Bien Hoa Airbase in Saigon. In a few hours the plane touched down and after a short wait at the airport, we all boarded a commercial jet for our R&R flight to Honolulu. I could not sleep during the flight and I could hardly wait to see Linda again. She had planned to fly to Honolulu the day before I got there and was now waiting for me to arrive. I was also looking forward to being out of Vietnam, if only for a week. The flight got to Honolulu and I reported to the R&R center at Fort DeRussy, where Linda was waiting along with many other anxious wives. It seemed strange seeing her again, but after a few hugs and kisses it seemed like we had never been apart. Unbelievably, the army had instructions and tips for us on how to enjoy our R&R, as if we could not figure it out for ourselves. Linda and I took a bus to our hotel, the Reef Lanai, which was very close to Waikiki Beach. We checked into the high-rise hotel and sat on our balcony talking and enjoying a wonderful view of

Honolulu. The week that both of us had looked forward to for so long had begun. Our first meal together in 11 months was steak and mahi-mahi, washed down by several glasses of wine. After a stroll through Honolulu after dinner, we headed back to our hotel to spend our first night together in almost a year.

Life's simple pleasures seemed special after 11 months in Vietnam. Most people take things like sleeping in a bed and hot showers for granted. Linda and I visited all the usual tourist attractions in Honolulu, including the International Marketplace, the zoo, and several historical sites. The souvenir shopping was great, and we strolled on Waikiki Beach and went swimming. We took a bus tour of the island and enjoyed the beautiful scenery and friendly people. I had been wanting to order a 35mm camera from the PX in Phu Bai but was not sure which one to get. After some advice from a guy in a camera shop in a large shopping center, I ended up ordering an Asahi Pentax, which I had for many years. Dinner was fabulous every night and we stayed up late, enjoying the nightlife. The entertainment in Honolulu was great and we even sat next to Johnny Rivers in one of the nightclubs. I could not believe how great it was to be out of Vietnam. The week went by and was over all too quickly; we had so much more to talk about. Leaving again seemed so final. Reluctantly, we went back to Fort DeRussy, where our time together came to an end and I prepared to head back to the war. After a difficult goodbye, I boarded a bus and headed to the airport for my flight back to Vietnam. Linda had to wait for her flight to Wisconsin and left the following morning. In eight short hours I was back in Phu Bai ready to resume the endless grind. Even though I had survived 11 months in Vietnam, I still had over two months left on my tour and things were getting hot in the Ashau Valley. I had plenty of time to worry about whether or not I would be returning home in July.

After I returned from R&R, the air war started to get intense and our Chinooks were receiving increasingly heavy anti-aircraft and automatic weapons fire in and around the Ashau Valley from concentrations of NVA troops. Charlie Company had an aircraft shot up badly by heavy machine-gun fire in the northern end of the Ashau Valley, and Bravo Company's aircraft 435 was destroyed and five crew members were killed. Flying was not much fun any more, and every time we left our base in Phu Bai, I wondered if we would return. My guts were in a constant knot.

I was flying on Pachyderm 541 during a mission in late April. We had just dropped off a load of ammo and other supplies on Firebase Ripcord and taken off from the mountain top. As the ship dropped down into a small valley in order to gain momentum, I heard the "rat-a-tat-tat, rat-a-tat-tat" of a machine gun opening fire. Before I had time to think, I heard the rounds smack into the bottom of the Chinook with a "bang, bang, bang" that sounded like somebody was beating the aircraft with a hammer. The Chinook's engines whined as we began to gain altitude, and the crew chief was screaming in his microphone, "We're being hit! We're being hit! Go, go, go!" With that, both of us opened up with our M-60s and sprayed the jungle below in an attempt to suppress the machine gun that was firing at us. We could not see where the rounds were originating from, but we kept firing anyway. Everything happened so fast that almost as soon as it started, it was over. We climbed higher before we leveled off and made our escape. The aircraft apparently had not taken any fatal hits and we were able to keep flying, so we headed back to the hangar in Phu Bai to check things out. The bottom of a Chinook was more or less impervious

Chinook over mountains near Firebase Ripcord.

to small-arms fire and the fuel tanks were self-sealing, so unless the engines, transmission, or the pilot took a direct hit, the big bird kept flying. When we got back to the compound in Phu Bai and landed, we were amazed when we counted 30 to 40 bullet holes in the bottom of the ship.

A few days later we were flying back to Phu Bai from somewhere in the Ashau. As we made our way along the river just west of Firebase Bastogne, I spotted a column of NVA moving along a trail near the river. I fired at them with my M-60, but we zipped past them so fast I could not tell if I hit any of them as they scattered into the brush. Eddie and I asked the aircraft commander if he would make

Author next to Chinook prior to flight.

another pass over the area so we could fire up the NVA. The pilot, who was one of the most experienced in the company, wisely said, "This is not a gunship." He continued flying back to Phu Bai and reported the NVA sighting to HQ on the radio. I knew the scenario that would follow. Within minutes Cobra gunships would rake the area with ARA and miniguns. Then a platoon or company of infantry grunts would assault the area to check for bodies and make further contact if the enemy was still in the area. I knew how the scenario worked because I had been involved in it at least a half-dozen times. Thankfully, I no longer had to participate.

On May 6, Firebase Henderson was attacked by the NVA. There were

45 airborne troopers and 29 enemy soldiers killed. Although I did not know it at the time, my old unit, Alpha Company, 2/501, was either on Henderson or in the vicinity. We flew out to the base the next morning, and on the mist-shrouded mountain top we picked up another cargo net full of bodies and body parts, including arms, legs and severed heads. As we lifted off with our grisly cargo, I could see still more dead NVA soldiers hanging in the wire surrounding the firebase. To this day I can still see the pile of mangled bodies we hauled off and smell the bloating corpses. It was not a sight most people would ever forget.

Thirteen days later, on May 19, Henderson was overrun by a battalion of NVA, and out of 37 Airborne troopers, only five survived. I was never able to get all of the facts, but I believe that my old unit was also involved and may have taken heavy casualties. The unit became known as "Hard Luck Alpha." That same day Pachyderm 526 was hit by enemy fire near Firebase Fuller, but the pilot was able to land safely not far from the firebase. Nobody was injured and the crew was extracted safely, but it had been touch and go for a while. An NVA force of unknown size tried to reach the downed ship, but it was driven off by a recovery force from Firebase Fuller that was sent to rescue the downed crew. The aircraft was later extracted and repaired.

A couple days later I went to the PX and ran into my buddy Larry, who was stationed just up the road with the 158th. He informed me that he knew for certain that three members of our old company had been killed somewhere near Ripcord or Henderson, but he was not sure of the details. Both the platoon leader and a squad leader from the 3rd Platoon were killed in action on February 20. Larry told me that the squad leader was walking point and ran into an NVA ambush. A .51 caliber machine gun had literally cut him in half. I was just sick to hear the news because both men were really great guys, and I remembered kidding around with the squad leader just before I left the company. The platoon leader had also been wounded earlier in a sapper attack. Another man in the company was killed in action on April 29, and I remembered that he had written "born" and his birth date, then "died" with a blank date on his helmet. I thought to myself, "Now he can fill in the blank." The news was like a punch in the gut, and I felt a mixture of sorrow for the loss of these fine young men and a tangible feeling of guilt for having left the company just before all the heavy fighting occurred.

Two nights later I was assigned to guard the main gate to the compound. I had an M-16 and walked back and forth near the gate, watching for anything suspicious. After about two hours I was startled by what appeared to be a man walking near the gate. I yelled "Halt!" but the man failed to stop and seemed to disappear into thin air. I was really freaked out by this and called the officer in charge to report my observation. He told me that I should have fired the man up, but I had not gotten a good look at him. I certainly did not want to risk hitting a civilian who might have been wandering around, even though civilians were forbidden to be near the base after dark. I never saw anything else that night and I was happy when the next gate guard arrived to relieve me. To this day I am not sure if I actually saw someone there or just imagined it. At the time, it was very real.

I was pretty numb the rest of my tour and I did everything I could to avoid reality and forget about Vietnam. The rest of May and June went by, and I don't remember a lot other than the usual routine of flight operations during the day and drinking at the EM club at night. Many of the guys in the 2nd Platoon smoked pot when they were not on duty; men in the 1st Platoon seemed to prefer alcohol. The two platoons were sometimes referred to as the "heads" and the "juicers." Any deviation from the daily grind of the war was a temporary escape from the boredom and a way to help forget the reality of Vietnam. I was in the 2nd Platoon with all my buddies, and I became part of a group of guys that sat out on the bunkers at night smoking pot and listening to music. On a couple of occasions somebody dipped a joint in liquid opium and let it dry before we smoked it. We called them "O-Js." That's as bad as it got for me, but there were a few guys who also did speed or acid now and then. I never wanted any part of that, nor did most of the other guys. The officers routinely conducted locker shake-downs and would often uncover somebody's stash of pot, but most of the time they winked and overlooked it. I had never used drugs of any kind while I was in college and almost nobody I knew in the infantry ever smoked pot or did any other drugs in the field. There was a common belief among many men, particularly those who smoked pot, that using pot still allowed them to function in emergencies, while men who were drunk were pretty much useless. I tended to believe that myself at the time, though I had no way of knowing if that perception was accurate. I now regret having been involved in the drug culture, if only for a very short time, but I also understand why I did it. I wanted to fit in with the rest of my buddies because they were all I had in Vietnam. They were my family then and none of us really knew for sure whether or not we would be going home. All of us were trying desperately to pass the time any way we could and to forget about the insanity and death all around us every day. I never got hooked on pot, and after I left Vietnam I never smoked again.

About two weeks before I was scheduled to process out of Vietnam and go home, my platoon sergeant took me off the flight roster. Short-timers were often taken out of the field a few weeks before they were scheduled to rotate back to the States. I was sent to the CO, and he asked if I wanted to extend my tour or re-enlist. I knew he had to ask, but I had a hard time keeping a straight face. Many of the men in the 159th actually did extend or re-enlist, but they had not been draftees and they had not spent eight months with an infantry platoon in the bush. I politely told the captain, "No thanks, I'm ready to go home and be a civilian again." He said, "I can't say that I blame you; good luck." I spent most of my remaining days assigned to what was referred to as "shit-burning" detail. This choice duty involved my removing the oil drum containers from under the latrines, pouring diesel fuel on the contents, and burning them. After a couple hours of work in the morning, I had the rest of the day off to read, lay in the sun, or go into Phu Bai. It was not the best duty the army had to offer, but it was far better than getting shot down just before I was ready to go home.

Finally, almost unbelievably, the time had come for me to leave Vietnam. On July 1, 1970, I said my goodbyes and hopped in a Jeep for the short ride to Camp Eagle, where I began to process out of Vietnam. There was a short medical exam, followed by paperwork to make sure I got paid and other routine forms that everyone who was processing out of Vietnam had to complete. I was issued the medals that I had earned — a Bronze Star, two Air Medals, and an Army Commendation Medal. The lines were long, but I didn't mind — I was going home! A supply clerk retrieved a duffel bag that I brought to Vietnam over a year earlier. It had been stored in a large warehouse and most of the clothes in it were moldy and smelled musty. I rifled through the bag and tossed everything except for my Class A uniform, a pair of jeans, and a couple of shirts.

The next morning several of us caught a flight on a C–130 cargo plane to Cam Rahn Bay, where we checked in for still more processing. I remember the barracks there were much nicer than anything I had lived in during my tour, and the latrines had sinks, running water, and real flush toilets. The mess halls were very nice and the food was good, but since this was a rear area I started to notice that some of the sergeants and junior officers were harassing us. On one occasion a young buck sergeant, probably right out of Fort Benning, came into our hootch and told us to report for sandbag detail. I remember that a large black soldier from the 1st Air Cavalry Division told the sergeant where he could put his sandbag detail. He apparently got the message, because he left abruptly without a word and did not return.

That night I took a walk along the beautiful white sand beach on the South China Sea and looked out at the peaceful water, thinking about home far across the Pacific Ocean. I could hardly believe that I would soon be there. I also thought a lot about what I had seen and experienced in Vietnam and thanked God that I had been so lucky. A whole year flashed across my mind as I sat there at peace with myself. I thought about the firefights, the helicopter flights, the verdant countryside of Vietnam, and the men who had died. Somehow I knew that I would never be the same person who had landed at Bien Hoa Airbase over a year earlier.

Finally, the paperwork was complete and the waiting game came to an end. I boarded a beautiful silver Freedom Bird and got ready to leave Vietnam along with over 100 other men. Heavy emotions and excited chatter filled the plane, but as it taxied down the runway and picked up speed to take off, it got very quiet. When the jet lifted off the ground, a loud cheer went up as everyone realized that the big day had finally come and we were going home! As the plane gained altitude and headed east over the Pacific, I reflected again on the 14 months I had just spent in Vietnam.

For me, the war was over. Or so I thought.

15

Welcome Home

When I left for Vietnam I weighed about 170 pounds. I was returning at least 30 pounds lighter. Like many veterans, I had the belief that once I got back to the United States everything would be great and all of my troubles would be over. I had dreamed of this day for over a year but did not realize that the America I had left was not the same and that I was not the same either.

Conflicting thoughts and emotions swirled in my head during the long flight home. I was overjoyed to be heading back to my family and the future seemed bright, but I had nagging thoughts of my buddies still in Vietnam. They were facing the rest of their tours of duty and potential injury or death. I thought about the war and whether or not it was worth all the lives that were being lost. I did not reach any conclusions. The flight home was very quiet and somber with many of the men contemplating the year they had just completed. Everyone seemed to be buried in private thought.

During our flight back to Fort Lewis we made one brief stop in Guam and had a little over an hour to wait while the plane refueled. Most of the guys stocked up on duty-free liquor, but I was not interested. After a brief look around the small terminal, I went back to my seat on the plane and stared out the window. I just wanted to get back to the United States, get discharged from the army, and go home.

The rest of the flight seemed to last for an eternity, but finally the pilot announced that we were on our final approach to Seattle-Tacoma International Airport. There was dead silence on the plane as men stretched to look out the windows for a glimpse of "the world." When the wheels of the plane touched down, all hell seemed to break loose as men cheered loudly and slapped each other on the back for several minutes. It was pandemonium. Most of us could hardly believe that we had finally made it home. The plane taxied down the runway toward the terminal, then came to a stop. When I looked out the window I didn't see anyone lined up to greet us—just MPs (military police) who quickly ushered us into the airport after we emptied the plane. We were searched for drugs and weapons, and I couldn't help thinking, "We just served our country for over a year and risked our lives, and now we are being searched like common criminals." After the hassle was over we boarded a bus for the ride to Fort Lewis where a steak-and-eggs breakfast awaited us. It was still early in the morning and dark, so I didn't see much on the way to Fort Lewis. When we got there, the breakfast was waiting for us as promised. A colonel in his dress uniform gave us the only welcome we would get. He droned on about the service we had just performed for our country and told us that we could be proud of ourselves. We were, but apparently the rest of the country was not. Excitement filled the air during breakfast, and men talked about their plans for the future now that Vietnam was in the past. Most of us did not realize that the war would remain an open wound for many years, and for some, the wound would never heal.

Unbelievably, we had still more paperwork to complete and ended up sitting with our duffel bags on the ground outside a large white building, waiting for our names to be called. An army of clerks reviewed our military records, verified our pay status, looked at our discharge papers, and briefed us on veterans' benefits. There was another very cursory physical, and we were asked if there were any injuries or conditions we wanted to report. In the same breath, we were told that reporting injuries or other medical conditions could delay our departure home by as much as a week. As far as I could tell, nobody reported anything. Finally, we visited the paymaster to report for our final pay in the army.

While we were sitting around as a group, a young second lieutenant came along and started to harass a couple of soldiers about not being shaved and not having haircuts. A captain who was sitting with the group got up and confronted the man, telling him "You're lucky one of these men doesn't kick your ass! You need to quit harassing men who have just come back from combat." The lieutenant apologized and left in a hurry, much to everyone's satisfaction.

I don't remember much else about processing out of the army other than the usual hurry-up-and-wait mode of operation. Somehow it finally ended early on July 7, 1970, and I was on a bus back to Seattle-Tacoma International Airport for my flight home to Wisconsin.

I arrived at the airport wearing my Class A uniform, which was adorned with my ribbons and the 101st Airborne Unit patch. It didn't take me long to figure out that wearing my uniform was a big mistake. We had been warned not to confront or argue with the anti-war protesters, but I really did not see anyone lined up with placards. Most people simply ignored me or glared at me, seeming to say, "What are you doing here?" One hippie girl stared at me as I stood trying to figure out where I needed to go in the airport, and I could see her mouthing obscenities at me. I was not naive enough to have believed that a brass band would be playing for my return, but I never expected or understood the deep hostility or the indifference that I would encounter.

I had some time to pass while I waited for my flight to Wisconsin, so I ducked into a small bar and ordered a beer. As I sat down, two people got up and moved away from me and left me sitting all by myself. When the long-haired bartender handed me the beer, he said, "Drink up and leave. You are bothering my customers and I don't want any trouble."

I was dumbfounded, and at first I didn't know what to say or how to react. I didn't say anything and after a quick swallow, I put my beer on the bar and left. I wanted yell, "What the hell is wrong with you people? Don't you know what I have just been through for this country?" I knew it was useless, so I left, feeling both angry and numb.

I walked down the hall in the terminal and sat down in an empty seat. As I sat there looking at my ticket and feeling hurt inside, I saw a small group of hippies sitting on the floor across the aisle from my seat. They were looking at me and whispering, then laughing. One of them made a face at me, and I wanted to go over and kick his stupid head in. Instead, I got up and left, not knowing how to react.

As I walked down the hall I was stopped by an airport security guard, who apparently had witnessed what had just happened. He said, "Ignore those goddamn hippies, they ain't worth crap. If you don't want to be hassled, though, you would be smart to change your uniform and put on your civilian clothes." I was really hurt inside but knew he was probably right, so I went into the men's room and dug out a shirt and pair of jeans from my duffel bag and changed clothes. The civilian clothes made me less of a target, but the short haircut and jungle rot scars on my arms were dead giveaways that I was just back from Vietnam. Other than stares and disgusted looks, I was not harassed any more and I boarded the plane for my flight.

We left Seattle and flew to Minneapolis, where I had to change planes for the short flight to Central Wisconsin Airport in Mosinee. Linda and my two boys were waiting for me there, and I could hardly wait to see them as I watched the green forests and farmlands of central Wisconsin pass by below. When the plane touched down on Wisconsin soil, I felt a tremendous sense of relief that I was finally home.

As I entered the airport terminal I immediately spotted Linda and ran up to her to give her a big hug and a kiss. Tim, who was now two years old, was dressed in a little blue outfit. He wanted no part of me as he peeked out from behind the seats, wondering who I was. I kept trying to pick him up, but he kept away from me. After I picked up my duffel bag, we went out to the parking lot and I got into our 63 Chevy Impala. It was the first time I had been behind the steering wheel of a car in over a year, and it felt great. On the ride home to our new apartment in Stevens Point, Tim kept asking Linda who I was and what I was doing there, talking loudly as if I were not there. Joe was just five months old, and this was the first time I had seen him. He was a chubby little rascal who seemed to smile a lot, and I had no trouble becoming his friend. It took at least a month before Tim gradually accepted me and understood that I was the dad he talked about to other people when he told them his daddy was in the army. It was wonderful to be home and everything seemed new to me.

After taking a day to get settled in, I decided to take a trip to Marshfield, where my parents lived. I wanted to surprise them because they did not know exactly when I was coming home. Linda and I had decided earlier to make my homecoming private.

After the short 35-mile trip, I pulled into the gravel driveway of the little house where I had grown up and walked up to the back door. I opened the door, went in without knocking, and entered the kitchen, where I saw my mother cooking something over the stove. She looked up and screamed "Johnny!" She hugged me for what seemed like 10 minutes in a very emotional mother-and-son reunion. I cannot really remember what we talked about, but I know that it was not Vietnam.

In about an hour my father came home from work and, after hugs and handshakes, we sat down to dinner. I cannot recall the exact nature of the conversation I had with my dad either, but it surely revolved around deer-hunting plans, trout fishing on the Tomorrow River, and bass fishing on Lake Emily. I do not recall either of my parents asking me much about Vietnam, and I did not volunteer any information. I was just so glad to be home that it did not matter.

That evening after supper I made plans to go out to one of the watering holes I frequented before I left for Vietnam. One of my college buddies who had not been in the military picked me up. We got to the bar, ordered beers, and traded small talk. Several guys who had gone to high school and played on the football team with me showed up and joined us at the bar. One of them was Mike, the guy who had been in basic training with me. He had just gotten back from Vietnam a few weeks before I did. Most of the conversation was juvenile, and an argument ensued about who had been the best running back on the football team. I really felt out of place and sat there politely listening to them argue about something that I no longer cared about. Nobody even mentioned Vietnam until one of the guys asked me in a loud voice, "So how many people did you kill over there?"

I was dumbfounded by his audacity and somehow avoided the question while I thought to myself, "You stupid jerk, I've just spent a year somewhere near hell and that's all you can think to say?" With that, Mike looked at me and read my mind. We both got up and left, headed for another bar, where we sat drinking beer and talking about Vietnam until the bar closed. We had stories to share and thoughts to sort out, all based on our common bond. I realized that my tour in Vietnam had changed me and that I had very little in common with my former friends. They were still locked into a high school or college mindset while I had been to war and had seen and experienced things that they could never understand.

Later that week my father-in-law, who was a World War II veteran, took me for a beer at a local tavern in his hometown and introduced me to several of his friends. Not much was said, just a polite hello, but no conversation about Vietnam. I was quickly learning that just about nobody wanted to talk about Vietnam, and I almost felt as if I had just returned from prison. I had just completed the adventure of my life and felt like I could not talk about it. Though most people showed no hostility toward me, it seemed like they were not interested and did not want to talk about Vietnam. Many years later Linda told me that she and most of the relatives were reluctant to bring up Vietnam because they thought that I did not want to discuss it. Maybe that was at least partly true.

The rest of the summer seemed to go by in a blur as I prepared to go back to college in the fall on the G.I. Bill. I went swimming and on picnics with Linda and the boys, and life was very sweet. I tried to forget all about Vietnam. Other than some nightmares and waking up to tell Linda she was on guard duty a few times, I began to put things in perspective.

Then one day in early September I got a call out of the blue from Eddie, the crew chief I had flown with in Vietnam. He had just gotten back and was passing through town and wanted me to meet him at a local restaurant. We greeted each other and exchanged small talk. He asked if I had heard about Jim, who had been in the 2nd Platoon with us. I told him that I had not heard any news from Vietnam since I left. He told me that Jim had been killed on Firebase Ripcord on July 18. I knew that Ripcord had been under steady attack from the NVA since early spring and that other Chinooks had been shot down near the firebase. Everyone was scared to fly there because the NVA had set up one or more 12.5mm anti-aircraft guns in the vicinity that could easily bring down a helicopter. Apparently a heavy attack had begun on July 1 with a mortar barrage. Bravo Company had an aircraft shot down by NVA ground fire and Pachyderm 495 was hit but was able to fly out safely. The next day Bravo lost another Chinook when an attempt was made to recover the aircraft that was shot down the previous day. Jim had been the flight engineer on Pachyderm 810 when it was hit by anti-aircraft fire while they were delivering supplies to Ripcord. The Chinook had crashed into the main artillery ammo dump and burst into flames. Jim had been trapped under the ship and burned to death. Over 400 artillery rounds exploded over the next few hours and all six of the howitzers on Ripcord were destroyed. On July 22 a Huey was shot down on Ripcord and the next day the base was extracted and abandoned after what had been a 23-day siege. During the extraction, Bravo Company lost another aircraft to enemy fire.

This news was really devastating, and Vietnam weighed heavily on my mind for several weeks. It was during this time that I took all the letters that I had written home to Linda, which she had carefully saved, and burned them one by one. I don't know why I did that; maybe I thought that getting rid of the letters would help erase the memories. One day, soon after the visit from Eddie, I was watching the latest news from Vietnam on television. I remember telling Linda that with the way Vietnamization was going, South Vietnam would fall to the North within five years. When South Vietnam fell in 1975, I was astounded at how accurate my prediction had been.

Fall came and I went back to college on a full-time basis, planning to get a second bachelor's degree, this time in biology. I could have gone back to Washington, D.C., and returned to my job with the Army Map Service, but I just could not cope with moving and felt that somehow school would be a fresh start.

It didn't take me too long to realize that I was not into school any more, and I had trouble concentrating on my studies. The daily news on TV never let me forget about Vietnam. The small campus in Stevens Point was not a hotbed of radical activity like the university in Madison, and I did not encounter any open hostility from the students. There were other Vietnam veterans in school, but I avoided joining any veterans' groups. I did not want to be reminded of the war, but that was very difficult with television news blaring the latest casualty figures every day. In some ways I wanted to talk about Vietnam, but I felt uneasy doing that and it was apparent that very few people wanted to hear anything from a former soldier.

Surprisingly, the only person who seemed to have any interest in Vietnam was a left-leaning sociology professor who opposed the war but never transferred that opposition to the soldiers or returning veterans. He asked me how things had been in Vietnam and wanted to know about my impressions, thoughts and opinions regarding the war. Talking to him was helpful, and he was one of very few people that I met who were the least bit interested in what I had experienced in Vietnam.

After a semester I realized that I was not cutting it in school. Besides, trying to make it financially on the G.I. Bill with a wife and two kids was pretty tough even though I worked most nights at United Parcel Service loading trucks. I quit school and applied for a job as an underwriter at a large insurance company in Stevens Point and was hired. The job was not particularly interesting to me, but it paid the bills and allowed us to get ahead a little financially.

While I was employed there, I did not experience any hostility toward me, maybe because few people knew that I was a Vietnam veteran. On several occasions in meetings, comments were made that indicated a reluctance by at least some of the underwriters to insure Vietnam veterans. On one occasion a smart-ass underwriter who couldn't have cut it in the military commented, "Most of these 'Nam vets are crazy dope addicts and we should not insure them." I had all I could do to keep from strangling the stupid jerk, and I let him know that I thought he was out of line. My comments to him made it obvious to the rest of the group that I was a Vietnam veteran. Surprisingly, nobody took my side of the argument. They remained silent.

In the fall of 1971, my father found out that he had incurable cancer, and I was devastated by the news. I had always been close to my father and tried to spend as much time with him now as I could. His health deteriorated steadily and he died in May, 1972. My mother told me that he sat up every night while I was in Vietnam, worrying and praying that I would return safely. I have no doubts that his prayers were at least partly responsible for my deliverance, and I felt so bad that I could not return the favor and keep him from dying.

Two years later I realized that I would never be happy working in the insurance business. I had been taking some night classes at the university and found out that I could earn a master's degree in natural resource management by attending just one full year to finish up the requirements. After careful consideration, I decided to go for it and left the insurance company to begin attending classes full-time.

In December, 1973, I earned a master's degree in Resource Management and in January I began my career as a soil scientist with the U.S Soil Conservation Service in Elko, Nevada. Within a year I transferred to the U.S Forest Service and had assignments during my career in California, Wyoming, and Montana.

Almost incredibly, I encountered some hostility toward veterans during my working career with the U.S. Forest Service. The U.S. Civil Service System awards veterans either a five- or ten-point veterans' preference in the civil service examination to help them in their pursuit of federal government employment. Often, veterans are at or near the top of the employment rosters and must be hired first. This requirement conflicted at times with another government policy dealing with affirmative action. The policy on affirmative action was to give hiring preference to females and racial minorities. Sometimes veterans were also females or minorities, and things worked out easily in those instances. On one particular occasion I heard a high-level personnel officer complaining because "veterans were plugging up the roster and didn't allow [her] to reach other females and minorities on the roster." In her opinion, the veterans' preference needed to go away. Another veteran and I were dumbfounded when we heard these statements. We both felt that anyone who had served their country in the military deserved no less than a small preference in getting hired. That was a pretty small price to pay someone who had given the government several years of service, often at great risk to their own safety.

I retired in 2002 from the position of Regional Soil Scientist in the Northern Region of the U.S. Forest Service in Missoula, Montana. Now I have plenty of time to pursue my hobbies of photography, writing, and fishing. Someday I hope to return to Vietnam to revisit the people and places that had such a huge impact and influence on the rest of my life.

On many occasions in the years since I returned from Vietnam I have realized how very lucky I was to have survived nine months of combat duty with a front-line infantry company, then five more months as a helicopter crew member flying over hostile territory almost daily. Though I did not suffer any physical wounds, I did not escape the psychological and spiritual wounds that are suffered by every man who has been in combat. In some ways, my experience with war and combat reminds me of the famous quote from the comic strip character Pogo, "We have met the enemy and he is us." For some, the war has never ended. For me, the war finally ended when I realized that only I could let it end.

16

Dreams and Illusions

Psychologists have known for a long time that new wars can cause old, repressed memories to come alive in veterans. The current war in Iraq is causing emotional stress and flashbacks for many Vietnam veterans. Some are experiencing even more serious problems, including PTSD (Post-Traumatic Stress Disorder). The guerrilla-style conflict, the mounting military and civilian casualties, and the political debate over the war are all vivid reminders of the conflict that occurred over 35 years ago in Vietnam.

Many people think of flashbacks as relived experiences that are so intense the person does not recognize the event as memory, but rather experiences it as something that is happening in "real time." While that is what happens to some who have more extreme flashbacks, most veterans, including myself, experience flashbacks as sudden, very vivid, recollections of past experiences or events that are usually triggered by sights, sounds, or smells. Sometimes it is difficult to separate flashbacks and memories from reality and put them in sequence. Often they are mere bits and pieces of faded memories.

Over the years since I returned from Vietnam, I have experienced flashbacks, just like many other veterans. These have not often been severe and are mostly repetitive and intrusive thoughts triggered by certain sights and sounds. The dreams are usually worse and are often very disturbing, but thankfully, they are infrequent. The following paragraphs describe several flashbacks and dreams that haunt me. The events are often scrambled, bits and pieces of reality that often turn surreal and become nightmares. Some events are based on my experiences and some are more illusory.

It had been raining all day and the overcast skies only added to my depressed feelings as I watched the evening news. More young GIs had been killed in Iraq, and I expounded about my feelings toward the war to Linda. She had no place to escape, so she listened quietly. After supper, I went for a walk with my dog Sadie, talking to her as if she understood what I was saying. After an evening of mind-numbing television programs I retired to bed, hoping to catch some much-needed sleep. I had a lot on my mind lately ... my son being deployed to Afghanistan, the war in Iraq. Finally, I drifted off to sleep ... *a military van pulls up in front of the house and two young sergeants stroll up to the door and knock. I answer the door, asking them what I can do for them. They answer by indicating that I should get dressed and get in the van.*

"Why?" I ask. "You have been drafted," one answers. I reply, "You must be joking. I am way too old to be in the military, and besides, I was already drafted once and served in Vietnam."

They tell me that it does not make any difference, that all men who have served before are being recalled and will be sent to Iraq since they already have experience. Over and over I protest, telling them that this is insane. They do not listen.

I am put on a bus with many other men about my age and almost instantly I find myself on patrol, walking along a darkened street with other men. I have a familiar object in my hands—an M-16 rifle.

As I walk along, I continue to protest what is happening but no words come out of my mouth ... all of a sudden Linda was shaking me, telling me to wake up. I sat up, and after a minute or so I realized that it was another dream. I was sweating and my heart was pounding, but I was relieved that it was not real. I tried to go back to sleep.

The August sun beat down on me as I sat on the bank of my favorite lake, hoping that I would be rewarded with a few nice trout for dinner. I became aware of a faint drone in the distance, getting closer and closer until I saw an aircraft headed straight toward me. As it drew closer, I could hear the "whop, whop, whop" getting louder until there was no mistake. It was a UH-1 Huey helicopter. As it roared overhead all kinds of thoughts raced through my mind and I continued to watch the Huey as it faded into the distance, finally disappearing over some distant hills. I both loved and hated that sound. My thoughts began to wander.... *Over the Huey's rotor and engine noise I hear the crew chief yell, "We're going in hot!" My gut tightens and my heart begins to beat faster as I look at the other squad members. All of them are craning their necks to look out of the open door at the jungle terrain passing below as they clutch their M-16s. Word has reached the aircraft commander that the first lift took AK-47 and machine-gun fire when they approached the LZ. One of the choppers had been hit but was able to continue flying and had inserted its troops onto the LZ. Heavy M-60 machine-gun fire from the other approaching Hueys had suppressed the enemy fire, at least temporarily. We hoped like hell the NVA had scrammed from the area around the LZ, but we knew better.*

As our lift circles and begins to approach the LZ, the door gunners open up with their M-60s and spray the treeline with heavy fire. I can see the barrels of their weapons getting hot and some of the ejected shells are landing inside where we are sitting. When we are about 20 feet above the ground we hear the AKs open up from the treeline. Several rounds hit and it sounds like somebody has hit the chopper with a sledge hammer. We try to make ourselves small and in no time we are jumping out of the open doors and hitting the ground. Nobody in the squad has been hit and we begin to return fire toward the treeline from behind the stumps that are shielding us from the enemy soldiers.

The second inbound chopper is not so lucky and we can see it trailing smoke as it sputters toward the LZ. It lands with a thump and we can see the crew and passengers bailing out as it bursts into flames. With that, two Cobra gunships appear and begin to strafe the treeline with ARA (aerial rocket artillery). The other two squads make it onto the LZ safely and we tentatively move toward the treeline to engage the NVA. We move slowly but do not get any return fire, and soon we are in the treeline. There are four dead NVA soldiers near a destroyed RPD machine gun. The ARA has done a job on them and there is blood and guts everywhere. A couple of the new cherries who just joined the platoon began to throw up when they see the carnage. We hear that two soldiers from the third squad were hit but not seriously. They are taken back to Camp Sally on the last chopper to land. After a brief rest and a smoke, we begin to move down a trail, toward an area thought to contain numerous NVA bunkers and ... a small trout hit my lure and I felt the rod bend as I began to bring him in to shore. The fish were starting to bite.

It was getting late but I continued to sort through some old photos of

Vietnam. I looked at the young guys in the photos, wondering if age had taken its toll on them as it had on me. There was a photo of Firebase Airborne that I took shortly after I joined Alpha Company in the Ashau Valley. I stared at the rows of concertina wire that surrounded the base and *... I see a red star cluster that somebody fired over the base and I hear somebody yelling, "Gooks in the wire, gooks in the wire!" Then I hear several loud explosions about 50 meters to my right as the nearest bunker position is hit with satchel charges. A couple of loud "ka-booms" signal, that the claymores are being blown and then one of the men hits the clacker for the fougasse drum. Its contents erupt with a loud "boom" as flaming napalm is sprayed over a wide section of the perimeter wire. M-16s and M-60s open up and continue firing toward the perimeter of the base. It is total bedlam with men yelling and many illumination flares going off along the bunker line. All of us in our bunker strain to see the NVA in the wire but we see nothing. Finally someone yells, "There's one," as he triggers our claymores. We all open fire and I drop several HE rounds from my M-79 grenade launcher into the wire as fast as I can fire and reload.*

After what seems like an hour but is only about fifteen minutes, somebody is yelling "cease fire" and things quiet down. There is only about an hour left before dawn and we all strain our eyes and search the bunker line nervously for any sign of further movement to our front. Nothing happens. Finally, it starts to get light enough to see and we gradually begin to make out several shapes in the wire. There are three or four badly burned corpses draped across the concertina wire and several more sprawled in the tanglefoot wire below. It has been a small probe by a squad of sappers. None of the men defending the bunker line has been hurt, but we know there will be further probes in the nights to follow. A squad of men prepares to go out and police up the dead bodies, which will be piled into a big cargo net. A Chinook will come to carry the carnage away. It is almost time to have some C-rations for breakfast and ... I snapped awake and put the photo album away. It was time to hit the sack and get some sleep.

The forest fire blazed out of control along the steep, forest-covered slopes of northern California. Several of us watched from a dirt road across the valley and wondered how long it would take before the blaze was under control. It looked like it would be a while. Then I heard a deep-pitched "whop-whop-whop" as a CH-47 Chinook helicopter made its way across the valley toward the blaze carrying a large water bucket suspended on a sling. As I watched it float across the valley.... *I can hear the crew chief yelling, "We're being hit, we're being hit!" The jet engines are screaming as the pilot maneuvers the big chopper, trying to gain altitude. It is too late. I can see red hydraulic fluid spraying all over the back of the chopper and the flight engineer is making his way forward rapidly, yelling something unintelligible over the din. The aircraft shudders and the engines whine as the pilot yells into his mike, "Hang on, we're going down!" We are not far off the ground now, heading for a small opening about 500 meters from the firebase we have just resupplied with ammo and C-rations. The pilot is able to auto-rotate and control the crash-landing, but we hit hard. Just like that, there is dead silence for a moment, then the pilot and co-pilot are scrambling out of the cockpit, asking if everyone is all right. Nobody seems to be hurt, but then several AK-47 rounds smack loudly into the side of the downed chopper. We exit the dead Chinook on the side away from the incoming rounds and hunker down, hoping that the grunts from the firebase will reach us before the NVA overrun the aircraft. We hear several more rounds hit as the AKs open up again. We return fire with the three M-16s we have on board and with the Colt 45 pistols the pilots carry. In the distance we can see a squad of grunts running toward. We keep firing toward the NVA, hoping the grunts will reach us in time....* I watched as the Chinook delivered its load of water onto the leaping flames and then banked sharply as it headed back to pick up another bucketful of water. I loved those big choppers, but they never failed to remind me of things that happened years ago.

About a month later that same year, I was hiking down into a distant valley with several other men. We were going to look at the feasibility of cutting timber in an area that one of the planners had marked on a topographic map. It was a typical hot California day and the sun was merciless as we struggled down the steep slope, fighting brush and mosquitoes. I looked around at the magnificent, tall Douglas fir trees as we struggled through sometimes impenetrable alder thickets and deerbrush. So much like the Ashau Valley, I thought to myself. Just ahead ... *I see movement near the trail and put my hand up to halt the column of soldiers following behind me. My slack man cautiously approaches behind me and whispers, "What's up?" I tell him that I think I saw some movement in the brush but was not sure what it was. We both peer at the brush in silence, hop-*

ing to see something, yet at the same time, hoping that we would not. Nothing moves, but we both have an eerie feeling because all of the usual noise and chatter from the birds and insects has gone silent. Something is up. With that the young lieutenant who has just taken over as platoon leader comes up and asks, "What's going on?" We inform him that we are not sure but suspect there might be an ambush set up ahead of us. He says, "I'm not taking any chances, let's call in artillery." The RTO, who had followed him up to our position, hands the lieutenant the handset as he checks our coordinates and calls in, requesting an artillery fire mission. We back down the trail about 200 meters and wait. In about two minutes we hear the artillery rounds approaching and wait for them to strike ... somebody was yelling "Look out by that stump! There's a big timber rattler coiled up there. Better give him a wide berth." We continued on to investigate the potential timber harvest area as I struggled with my private thoughts and distant memories.

The sun was setting over the Pacific Ocean as I headed back to Eureka after mapping soils in the Six Rivers National Forest all day. It had been a scorcher inland and I was looking forward to parking my truck in the motor pool and getting home for a late dinner. I made my way through sparse traffic in town and reached the compound. I got out of the truck to unlock and open the large chain link gate and ... *I peer out into the blackness beyond the main gate and look for any signs of movement. I thought I had heard something moving in the tall grass beside the main road, but I did not see anything. Probably some dog, I thought, as I looked around behind me to reassure myself that all of the big Chinook helicopters parked there at night were safe. I am all alone at the gate until midnight, when someone will come to relieve me from guard duty. What was that? I know I heard something again, maybe some kids fooling around. I yell "Di Di Mau!— Get out of here!" but nothing happens. Then I see it! A face— a Vietnamese face— seeming to float toward the front gate. I yell but the face keeps floating toward me, smiling. The eyes are hollow and vacant, as if they are not alive, and I scream but nothing comes out of my mouth. I begin to fire my M-16 at the face then....* I removed the lock and opened the gate, then drove my truck to its assigned place in the motor pool. I took my lunch box and headed for my own truck, somewhat shaken. Why did that gate remind me of another gate that I did not want to remember? All I wanted was to get the hell out of there and go home.

It was autumn, 1985, and elk hunting season in Wyoming had just begun. Both of my sons and I had waited all summer for this day and had spent weeks preparing equipment, reading reports, anticipating. The weather was unseasonably warm for mid–October and there was no snow yet as we packed the Jeep and prepared for an early start the following morning. At 0300 hours my sons were both awake and dressed already. They were anxious and urged me to hurry up and finish my coffee so we could get started. After a last-minute inventory of our gear, we jumped into the Jeep and headed for the Bighorn Mountains. There was a spot we had scouted and we thought there would be elk in the area. By 0400 we parked the Jeep at the trailhead and silently shouldered our daypacks. We loaded our rifles and made our way up a narrow trail toward a distant mountain ridge. In thirty minutes we were at a junction in the trail, and as we had planned, Tim and Joe split from me and began climbing a steep slope toward the ridgeline. I began to move slowly below them through some aspens and alders, hoping to spook any elk that were feeding there, driving them up toward the boys. Daylight was still about an hour away. The narrow trail wound back and forth through the thick stand of young trees and brush, and I moved along slowly. It was still very dark and I swore as I scratched my face on some low-hanging branches, then tripped on a root and fell flat on my face. After I got back up I stood silently trying to get my bearings and listening for the sounds of elk moving through the underbrush.

As I began to move along the trail again, I started to become uneasy for an unknown reason. As an experienced outdoorsman, I had done this many times before. I was not afraid of the dark, yet there was some unseen presence that I seemingly felt, and the hair on the back of my neck stood up. I began to sweat and then thought I saw someone coming down the trail ahead of me. I was surprised since there had been no other vehicles parked at the trailhead and I thought we were alone. I called out, not wanting to startle the man, and he seemed to disappear.

I was puzzled and became more and more nervous and confused. Then I heard some movement in the brush to my left and I froze. At first I thought it was an elk, but then I realized that the sound was too faint to be such a large animal. Could it be a mountain lion stalking me, I wondered. I scanned the area and saw nothing at first, then through the fading darkness.... *I saw three other men but they were not on the trail. They had on backpacks and were wearing pith helmets. Then I knew who they were—NVA!* I knew I was not dreaming and I was wide awake. I thought to myself, "This is bullshit, it ain't real!" With that, the figures disappeared and I started to shake. I was almost in a state of panic but managed to keep myself under control, and I resisted the urge to run back down the trail. I decided to sit against a large aspen tree and wait for it to get light enough to see before I did anything. After about 30 minutes it was beginning to get light and I could see well enough to make out a small herd of deer silently moving up the hillside about 40 meters ahead of me. Could they have been what I saw? No way, I thought. I definitely saw gooks with pith helmets, yet I knew they were not really there. I was so shaken that I decided to return to the Jeep and wait for the boys to return later that morning. On my way back I met a couple of other hunters on the trail and they asked if I'd seen anything. "Naw," I replied. "Just a few deer heading up the mountain. Don't think there's much in this area." After I got back to the Jeep I poured myself a cup of coffee from the Thermos on the front seat and sat there staring out the window. I was upset with myself for not continuing on the trail, and I realized what had happened. The darkness, the heavy brush, and the silence had all combined to create one of the most vivid flashbacks I had ever experienced. I tried to think about elk hunting but could not. My hunt, for that day at least, was over. Later that morning the boys came back down the trail and joined me. I could not tell them what had happened to me. As we shared a cup of coffee I asked if they'd seen any elk. "Nope," they replied. "Let's try another area."

After more than 35 years, the intrusive thoughts and the visions of a war long since over still remain, but they have dimmed. I feel lucky, though, compared to many others. Bad memories seem like a small price to pay. Many other men paid a much higher price. Like many other soldiers, however, the dreams still haunt me.... *The early morning is already hot and steamy as I look around the small clearing in the jungle, somewhere near the Ashau Valley. I see spectral images in the thick underbrush and I hear them slowly creeping up the hill toward me. They are NVA and their hollow eyes look right through me as though I am not real. Slowly they vanish into the mist and retreat into the past as I awaken in a cold sweat. They are ghosts, only ghosts.*

Epilogue

Writing this book has been difficult for me, but it was something that I had to do. It forced me to think about events and to dredge up thoughts that I had buried in my mind long ago. At times the recollection of those thoughts and events was intense. I had trouble sleeping and suffered an episode of temporary amnesia, which caused me to be hospitalized for two days.

I have attempted to portray Vietnam as it was for me and to give the reader some sense of what it was like to have served in a front-line combat infantry unit, even though there were no front lines. As I wrote this book, it became clear to me that it was impossible to completely and accurately convey with words all of the sights, sounds, smells and the feelings that were Vietnam. Even today when I listen to the music from the '60s and '70s I often find myself back in Vietnam. When I hear music by the Doors, Creedence Clearwater Revival, Three Dog Night, Blind Faith and many more groups, I can't avoid thinking about places in Vietnam and events that occurred more than 35 years ago. Sometimes I can almost feel the heat and humidity and hear the jungle sounds. I remember the weight of my rucksack digging into my shoulders as I struggled up a steep jungle trail. When I look at the often fog-shrouded mountains in northern Idaho, I think of the mountainous terrain around the Ashau Valley in Vietnam. When I hear a helicopter fly over, the "whop, whop, whop" of the rotor always brings back memories that I'd like to forget. Memories from so long ago and so far away.

Sorting out my thoughts and recollections made me realize that the

14 months I spent in Vietnam have had a profound effect on me and in many ways have defined my life, for better and for worse. Although I am a spiritual person, my devotion to formal religion began its gradual death in the Southeast Asian jungle. I still have a vague sense of guilt for having returned safely when so many others did not. In spite of my mixed feelings about the war and what it did to me and many others, I am glad that I served my country in Vietnam and if I had to do it all over again, I would. I am especially proud to have served in the 101st Airborne Division, one of the best and most famous military units in the world.

The American military was not defeated in Vietnam; public opinion turned against the war and Congress voted to end United States involvement. The fighting ended after an agreed stalemate, and a peace treaty was signed in Paris by the United States, South Vietnam, North Vietnam, and the Viet Cong on January 27, 1973. It called for the release of all U.S. prisoners, withdrawal of U.S. forces, limitation of both North and South Vietnamese forces inside South Vietnam, and a commitment to a peaceful reunification of both countries. The last American troops departed from Vietnam on March 29, 1973, and 590 U.S. prisoners of war were released. On January 8, 1975, North Vietnam violated the agreement and began a major invasion of South Vietnam. President Ford and the United States did not intervene, and on April 30 South Vietnam fell to the Communists, two years after the American military left Vietnam.

Over 58,000 U.S. forces were killed in action in Vietnam; 35,000 of those casualties were army and marine infantry soldiers and 3,000 were helicopter crew members. Of the 2.8 million men who served in Vietnam, fewer than 10 percent served in infantry units. Over 80 percent of all U.S. casualties however, were suffered by men in the infantry. These men had a greater than 10 percent chance of being killed or seriously wounded during their 12-month tour of duty.

Many draftees ended up in the infantry, and in 1969–1970 over 40 percent of the soldiers killed in action were draftees. The infantry, as in all wars, suffered a disproportionate number of killed and wounded during the fighting. As bad as United States losses were, the Vietnamese suffered even heavier casualties. About 224,000 South Vietnamese troops were killed in action, as well as over a million North Vietnamese and Viet Cong troops. Ho Chi Minh had said, "You can kill ten of my men for every one I kill of yours, but even at those odds, you will lose and I will win." He was right.

The 101st Airborne Division suffered the third highest number of men killed in action (4,022) in Vietnam. Only the 1st Air Cavalry Division and the 25th Infantry Division lost more men. Thua Thien Province in I Corps, where I served for 14 months, had the highest number of U.S. Army personnel killed in action in Vietnam.

Should the United States have gone to war in Vietnam? I did not think so when I was in college or after I was drafted. Our reasons for being there centered around the domino theory, which stated that if Vietnam fell to communism, the rest of Southeast Asia would follow. Ultimately, that theory proved to be false; no other countries fell to communism. Over the years, however, I have become more inclined to believe that our presence there may have served both a geopolitical and a humanitarian purpose. At least I want to believe that. Whether or not the United States should have been involved can still be debated, but for me that question is one for historians to decide. In fact, we were involved and I fervently believe that the sacrifices made by so many veterans did have meaning and did serve a noble purpose.

Unlike soldiers today, most Vietnam veterans went to war alone and returned home alone. Most fought for their buddies and the right to return home, not for some lofty political ideal. Like veterans who fought in wars before Vietnam, we were affected in many ways. The awful treatment received by many Vietnam veterans who returned from an unpopular war is the one thing that distinguishes them from veterans who served in World War II, Korea, and now in Afghanistan and Iraq. Both of my sons are career navy personnel, and I was so proud of them and happy to see the honorable treatment they received when they returned from the 1990 Gulf War. I am very happy that the military veterans returning from Iraq and Afghanistan are receiving the honor they so richly deserve.

Sadly, I still remember the shameful treatment that many of us received when we returned home from Vietnam. We were visible reminders of an unpopular war and we became little more than detritus to be swept under the rug and relegated to the scrap heap of history. Recent attempts to welcome Vietnam veterans home are a little late. Like many other Vietnam veterans, I have a special contempt for those who deserted our country and for the Hollywood actress who gave aid and comfort to the enemy by going to Hanoi during the war and dishonoring her country. There is a big difference between those who legitimately disagreed with United States government policy and those who were cowards and traitors. Hopefully, there was at least one important lesson learned from the Vietnam war: It is acceptable to disagree with government policy on a war but not to blame the veterans who serve their country.

Several years ago I was in Washington, D.C., on business, and decided to visit the Vietnam Veterans Memorial. I hardly noticed the people who were moving around me as I slowly walked along the wall. I was oblivious to my surroundings as my mind wandered back to Vietnam. When my thoughts returned to the present all I could do was shed silent tears; so many had died.

Glossary

Agent Orange: An herbicide containing trace amounts of the toxic contaminant dioxin that was used during the Vietnam War to defoliate areas of jungle growth.

Air Medal: Awarded for meritorious achievement while participating in aerial flight, either as an aircraft crew member or as an infantryman participating in an aerial combat assault.

Airmobile: Helicopter-borne combat personnel from the 101st Airborne Division and the 1st Air Cavalry Division.

AIT: Advanced individual training, sometime advanced infantry training.

AK-47: The automatic 7.62mm assault rifle used by the Viet Cong and North Vietnamese.

AO: Area of operations.

APC: Armored personnel carrier.

ARA: Aerial rocket artillery.

Arc Light: A B-52 air strike. Normally at least three aircraft carrying about 108 bombs each.

Army Commendation Medal: Awarded for heroism, extraordinary achievement or meritorious service.

ARVN: Army of the Republic of (South) Vietnam.

Ashau Valley (also spelled A Shau): Near the Laotian border, one of the main entry points into South Vietnam of the Ho Chi Minh Trail. It was an area critical to the NVA and Viet Cong for the movement of troops and supplies into I Corps. Because of this, the valley and surrounding mountains were targets of many operations by allied forces, especially the 101st Airborne Division. The area acquired a fearsome reputation and was the scene of the famous battle for Dong Ap Bia (Hamburger Hill).

Glossary

Battalion: An organizational army unit commanded by a lieutenant colonel. An infantry battalion usually had about 900 men but was often smaller due to casualties.

Blivet: Large rubber bladder used for transporting and storing fuel or water.

Boonies or Bush: Term used for the field or jungle.

Bush Hat: Floppy olive drab hat worn in the rear and on night ambush missions instead of the heavy steel helmet.

Bronze Star Medal: Awarded for heroic or meritorious achievement or service while engaging enemy forces.

C4: A very stable plastic explosive carried by infantry soldiers, usually used for clearing helicopter landing zones (LZs). It could be safely burned and was used by soldiers to heat water and C-rations.

C-130: A four-engine, high-wing cargo plane used for hauling troops and supplies. It could take off and land on unimproved landing strips.

C-Rations: Canned rations carried by troops in the field.

CA: Combat assault. An assault by infantry troops from helicopters.

Cherry: A new troop replacement.

Chi Com: Chinese communist. Many of the North Vietnamese claymores and grenades were of Chinese origin.

Chieu Hoi: Literally, "Open Arms." South Vietnamese government program that encouraged enemy soldiers to defect. Many served as scouts for American infantry platoons.

Chinook: The CH-47 twin-rotor helicopter used to transport equipment and troops.

Claymore: A small antipersonnel land mine used for perimeter defense and for setting up ambushes. Each infantry soldier carried one or more claymores in the field.

CO: Commanding Officer.

Cobra: The AH-1G helicopter gunship. The cobra carried rockets, mini-guns and a 40mm gun in a turret under the nose of the aircraft.

Combat Infantryman Badge (CIB): Awarded to members of infantry and special forces units for active involvement in ground combat.

Company: A military unit commanded by a captain and consisting of two or more platoons, 250 men at full strength.

Concertina Wire: Coiled razor wire used as part of the perimeter defense around most firebases and secured areas in Vietnam.

Contact: Engagement with the enemy.

CP: Command Post.

Crew Chief: The air crew member in charge of fueling and maintenance on a helicopter. He also served as a door gunner.

Dap: A complex, ritual handshake often used by black soldiers.

Det Cord: A thin flexible tube loaded with explosive used as a fuse or wrapped around a tree with C4 to fell the tree in clearing landing zones.

Dong Ap Bia: Mountain on Laotian border, also known as Hamburger Hill.

Door Gunner: The air crew member in charge of maintaining and operating the M-60 machine guns aboard a helicopter. They were so named because the gun position was usually in the open door of the aircraft.

Drill Instructor (DI): Sergeant in charge of basic training of new recruits.

DMZ: The demilitarized zone between North and South Vietnam.

Eagle Beach: 101st Airborne Division R&R area on the South China Sea.

Elephant Grass: Tall, sharp-edged grass found in the highlands of Vietnam.

F-4 Phantom: Jet fighter-bomber used in Vietnam.

Firebase (FB) or Fire Support Base (FSB): Temporary to semi-permanent artillery firing position used to support infantry troops in the field. These bases dotted the Vietnam landscape and usually consisted of several 105mm and 155mm howitzers and their crews on a hilltop, surrounded by an infantry company.

Firefight: Small-arms fire exchange with an enemy force.

Flak Jacket: A heavy, fiberglass-filled vest worn for protection. These vests were heavy and hot, and many units in the 101st Airborne Division did not wear them in the field.

Fougasse: 55-gallon drum filled with napalm and C4 used as a defensive weapon on firebase perimeters. When detonated, they sent out a wall of flames.

Frag: A fragmentation grenade. Each infantry soldier carried anywhere from two to six grenades, depending on the mission.

Freedom Bird: The aircraft that takes a soldier home at the end of his tour of duty. It was usually a civilian contract aircraft.

Friendly Fire: Any air, artillery or small-arms fire from one American position mistakenly directed at another American position.

Gook: Derogatory term for Vietnamese and other Asians.

Green Tracers: Color of enemy tracer rounds. American tracer rounds were red.

Grunt: An infantry soldier.

HE Round: High explosive round for the M-79 grenade launcher.

Hootch: Barracks or living quarters.

Hot LZ: A landing zone where helicopters are receiving enemy weapons fire.

Hue: The old Imperial capital of Vietnam and the largest city in Thua Thien Province.

Huey: The UH-1 helicopter, often called a Slick. This helicopter was a workhorse used to transport and insert troops, carry supplies, and perform medical evacuation.

HQ: Headquarters

I Corps: The northernmost of four military regions in South Vietnam.

Incoming: Receiving enemy mortar or rocket fire.

Jungle Boots: U.S. combat boots that had uppers made mostly of green canvas-like material that did not rot as quickly as leather. They also had a metal shank in the sole that offered some protection against sharp objects.

Jungle Penetrator: A metal cylinder lowered by cable from a helicopter to extract personnel from a site inaccessible to the helicopter.

KIA: Killed in action.

Kit Carson Scout: A former NVA or VC who performed scout duties for the U.S. military.

Klick: A kilometer.

LAW: M-72 light antitank weapon. This shoulder-fired 66mm rocket was often used against enemy bunker complexes.

Log Bird: A logistics (resupply) helicopter.

LOH: OH-6A light observation helicopter (Loach).

LP: Listening post. Usually a two- or three-man post outside the wire surrounding a firebase. The men would stay hidden and take turns during the night listening and looking for enemy movement, serving as early warning for troops inside the wire. These positions were very vulnerable if discovered by the enemy and could be inadvertent targets for friendly fire.

LT (El Tee): A lieutenant.

Lurp Rations: Freeze-dried rations very similar to backpackers' meals. Usually much tastier and preferred to C-rations, but having enough water to hydrate the meals was often a problem.

LZ: Landing zone. A clearing large enough to land at least one helicopter.

M-16: The standard 5.56mm assault rifle used by American troops in Vietnam.

M-60: The standard 7.62mm machine gun used by American troops in Vietnam.

M-79: Single-shot grenade launcher which fired 40mm high explosive, illumination and buckshot rounds. Also called a thumper because of the hollow "thump" sound it made when fired.

Mad Minute: Concentrated fire of all weapons for a brief time. Often done at predetermined times on firebases to keep potential enemy sappers off guard.

Medevac: Medical evacuation helicopter, also called a dust-off.

MIA: Missing in action.

Minigun: 7.62mm Gatling-style machine gun that could shoot 6,000 rounds per minute.

Napalm: Highly combustible jellied gasoline. Usually dropped from the air, it stuck onto its target and burned intensely.

NCO: Non-commissioned officer.

NDP: Night defensive position.

Nuoc Mam: Fermented fish sauce used by the Vietnamese. Its pungent odor permeated the air around Vietnamese villages and cities.

NVA: North Vietnamese Army or a soldier in that army.

OCS: Officer Candidate School.

One-Five-Five: 155mm howitzer.

One-O-Five: 105mm howitzer.

OP: Observation Post.

Phu Bai: City in Thua Thien Province, headquarters for the 101st Airborne Division.

Platoon: A military unit composed of about 40 personnel, commanded by a Lieutenant.

Point Man: The lead soldier in a patrol. His job was to lead the patrol safely while watching for enemy booby traps and ambushes.

Poncho Liner: Light nylon quilt used as bedding in Vietnam.

Punji Stakes: Sharpened bamboo stakes embedded in the ground, designed to penetrate the foot or leg of anyone walking into one.

R&R: Rest and recreation. Every soldier in Vietnam was authorized a seven-day R&R during his tour of duty.

RIF: Reconnaissance in force.

ROKs: Republic of Korea soldiers.

RPG: Soviet bloc-made rocket-propelled grenade fired from an antitank rocket launcher.

RTO: Radiotelephone operator, the man who carried the platoon's radio.

Rucksack or Ruck: The aluminum-framed backpack carried by infantry troops in the field, often loaded with 70 to 80 pounds of equipment, ammunition, food and water.

Sampan: A small wooden boat used by the Vietnamese.

Sapper: Elite NVA/VC commandos trained to penetrate defensive perimeters and set demolition charges to blow up bunkers, ammo dumps and command posts, usually prior to a ground assault by enemy infantry.

Satchel Charge: Explosive charge usually carried in a canvas bag. The chief weapon used by sappers.

Screaming Eagles: nickname for the 101st Airborne Division.

SERTS: Screaming Eagle Replacement Training School. Rear-area indoctrination course for newly arrived 101st Airborne Division replacements.

Short-timer: A soldier who was "short" (near the end of his tour of duty in Vietnam).

SITREP: Situation report. A radio transmission from a field unit to report that unit's current status.

Slackman: The second man in a patrol, backup to the point man.

Squad: A military unit of about 12 personnel, commanded by a sergeant.

Stand Down: A period of rest and resupply after completing a field mission.

Starlight Scope: A night vision scope that utilizes outside light sources for illumination. Often used on firebase bunker lines to scan the perimeter.

Stars and Stripes: The official U.S. military newspaper, often delivered to field troops with resupply.

Tanglefoot: Barbed wire staked low to the ground to prevent enemy sappers from crawling.

Thua Thien: A province in northern I Corps, Vietnam.

Thumper or Thump Gun: Nickname given the M-79 grenade launcher.

TOC: Tactical operations center.

VC: Viet Cong. South Vietnamese communist guerrillas.

Vietnamization: The plan by President Nixon to turn the war over to the South Vietnamese military while the United States withdrew from the conflict with honor.

WIA: Wounded in action.

World, The: The United States, home, or anywhere other than Vietnam.

Index